Children w
before t

Children who communicate before they are born

Conversations with unborn souls

Dietrich Bauer
Max Hoffmeister
Hartmut Goerg

TEMPLE LODGE

Translated from German by Pauline Wehrle

Temple Lodge Publishing
Hillside House, The Square
Forest Row, RH18 5ES

www.templelodge.com

First published in English by Temple Lodge 2005

Originally published in German under the title *Gespräche mit Ungeborenen, Kinder kündigen sich an* by Verlag Urachhaus 1986

A catalogue record for this book is available from the British Library

ISBN 1 902636 68 6

Cover by Andrew Morgan
Typeset by DP Photosetting, Aylesbury, Bucks.
Printed and bound by Cromwell Press Limited, Trowbridge, Wilts.

Contents

Foreword

There is hardly a day goes by without the themes of this book being drawn to our attention, either as headlines in the press, or as a series of programmes on television. On the one hand, we hear about all the advances in the science and technology of conception and birth, including progress in 'in-vitro' techniques, repro-genetics and, last but not least, cloning and our potential to reproduce human beings in a way that does not belong to the biology of higher animals, including man, at all. On the other hand, we hear about all the human questions that arise out of all this, along with the heartache and desperation in the face of the increasing infertility in the western world. And, most of all, we hear about the ethical and moral questions that are growing in complexity as these technologies advance and differentiate. Interestingly, the issue of abortion, legal in this country, rarely makes the headlines, although there are signs of growing concern here as well.

This book, which was published in 1986, might seem to be outdated. The birth technologies were then in their infancy, and it is the question of abortion that is most intensely discussed. The legislation to which the book refers (pp. 87–90) was put in place in Germany in 1974 and much has happened since then. But the fundamental dilemma is the same now as it was then, and it is the dilemma of human rights. The so-called 'paragraph 218' in the German legislation states the right of every human being to self-determination. In this country we know this in a perhaps more existential form, as the growing conviction that each person has a right to decide what is 'best' for their own life – and that includes the right to abort an unwanted child. Any obligation to the unborn child is for many people secondary to their right to self-determination. This is a failure of imagination, which comes from the problem at the very heart of this issue. The problem can be stated in this way!

If one looks at the development of the child in the womb with all the techniques available today, then one can only go back as far as conception, for that is the first sense-perceptible presence of the future human being. From conception onwards, the facts of development are well known because the embryo can be *seen* to grow and metamorphose, until it begins to have something like a recognizable human form, i.e. at 3–4 weeks, still for the most part unknown to the mother, unless she is very sensitive to her own body. But there is a question that cannot be answered if one looks at embryological development simply in this way. One cannot know when the soul comes into being, when someone is there, a person, in that tiny, fragile growing form. There is much speculation over this with very little ability to come to an objective conclusion. The soul of man is always invisible. It only *seems* to be visible from birth onwards because it animates, gives 'anima', to the body. The very early human embryo has no such discernible animation and it can easily be seen as nothing more than a biological process, driven by DNA, and not too different from mammalian embryology in general. The more materialistic scientists can give many facts that point to the simply biological. And those who have a more religious bearing on the subject cannot give enough objective substance to their convictions. The result of this is clear for us all to see. If we do not *know* anything for sure, then we can *do* anything because nothing is standing in the way. The present mushrooming of the birth technologies comes out of not knowing on the one hand and, on the other, out of a sincere wish on the part of most of the medical and scientific communities to help people.

Helping people is, of course, all to the good, but to do so without perceiving something of the bigger picture will bring problems.

The real remedy for this situation is to bring this bigger picture into focus. This is not easy to do within the modern scientific culture that demands, in the words of St Luke's Gospel, 'proof of spirit'. Proof of that kind cannot be given since it is impossible to prove the existence of one realm with the methods of another. Proof of pre-birth existence is essentially not available to the methods of natural science.

There is, however, a method that can begin to open up this realm even for the consciousness of today if it is not too reductionist and can remain open. It is the method that can be called 'phenomenology' and it is the one used in this book by Bauer, Hoffmeister and Goerg. *Children who communicate before they are born, Conversations with unborn souls;* the title describes the method. The authors have collected stories from young children, their parents, friends and those in the medical profession who have something to tell—in children it is from direct memory, and parents (mostly mothers) have had either sleeping or waking dreams about their unborn child. All of this can be seen as some kind of hallucination or a reflection of subjective wishes without reality. This was the first response of doctors and scientists to the accounts given of the other end of life—by those people who had near-death experiences. More and more doctors are now coming to the conclusion that the NDE cannot be discounted on purely materialistic grounds. The phenomenology is beginning to speak for itself. The climate of opinion is slowly changing, at least in relationship to the possibility of the survival of the soul after death. If there is to be the same kind of openness to the possibility of pre-birth existence then a major hurdle has to be jumped. All near-death experiences describe the survival of an individual, a human being who recognizes himself in that space as the same person as before, on this side of the threshold. To do the same, to accept that it is an individual, a person, who exists before birth, and not simply a drop of God's Being, is much more difficult. It would imply the possibility of reincarnation. All the accounts in this book suggest that it is a person who communicates before birth. There is someone there, after death and before birth, and the spirit is a continuity.

A great deal, however, is changing. One can begin to see how effective phenomenology can be. Recently in the USA, where there is a battle between the 'Pro-choice' groups and the 'Pro-life' groups, many women who are considering an abortion changed their minds on seeing ultrasound pictures of their unborn children. The *reality* of the unborn has been brought home to them and they can begin to see a reality beyond that centred on themselves. This book helps to bring this reality to consciousness. It is an important event that it is now published in English and will be available to many more people. The language of the book is highly accessible, needing neither the details of natural science nor of spiritual science to be understood. The pictures can speak for themselves.

Pearl Goodwin
Stourbridge, March 2005

DIETRICH BAUER

'I want to be born now'

Introduction

From time immemorial human beings have been stirred by the mystery of the arrival of children. Myths and fairy tales, descriptions in religious documents, legends and stories all draw our attention to the exalted and sacred nature connected with human birth. If as modern people we have preserved enough sensitivity we can hardly fail to feel the magic of a birth and early childhood, especially if this occurs in our near neighbourhood. If we listen responsively to reports by expectant mothers of the feelings that fill them with anticipation of the arrival of their child, we are frequently aware of a very delicate but absolutely real connection between the mother and her unborn baby, often in fact to a soul not yet conceived. We are told about profoundly impressive dream experiences, of visions of light, tremendous images of clouds, rainbows or water, or of mighty voices, occurring in connection with the announcement of the coming child. Sometimes the mother experiences a vivid picture of the disposition and character of the child, sometimes she experiences its appearance or its name. She is absolutely certain that the being of the child is in existence before conception.

In the light of the fear of overpopulation and the problems concerned with abortion litigation in connection with the possibilities of human choice (e.g. artificial insemination), it is an extremely burning issue that we deepen our thoughts on birth.

In the controversy over paragraph 218 (see pp. 87–90) there are still two opposing, unreconciled points of view. One view believes it to be a monstrous crime that abortion, considered earlier on as murder, should now be thought of as an almost obvious right of the living vis-à-vis the unborn. Leading the way, the Pope [John Paul II] repeatedly states his support for 'unborn life'. The opposite point of view is that people's rights still do not go far enough. Some women, in the fight to gain total freedom of choice for or against the life which is on the way, wage war under the motto 'my tummy belongs to me'.

There are also extremely divergent ways of regarding the population problem. Why are people in Germany — and more or less in all industrialized nations — so anti-children, where it would be a relatively easy matter after all for many of the families to feed more children? And why, where the foundations of life are limited and fear of starvation is the order of the day — in the so-called Third World — do so many children nevertheless come into the world that the relevant governments will often turn to any means of reducing their number?

The most staggering fact about all these discussions is the poverty-stricken nature of the arguments. For what comes to light here is not only the underlying power of volition but the lack of respect for the human being inherent in our materialistic world conception, and which for centuries, and especially strongly in recent decades, has found its way deeply into our hearts. This is the reason for the very large-scale loss of a real connection between the world as such and ourselves as human beings. The thoughts engendered by extreme materialists have become our common property and the essential quality of our feelings.

Are there really no viewpoints today which could serve as a basis for looking at the problems of birth control, abortion, even artificial insemination, in a way which could bring us to a secure, humanly dignified outlook? Is 'human propagation' in fact governed solely by the one chance in a million or, at best, human, all-too-human choice? In this present book mothers and fathers and also friends of the family are given the chance to speak. They give accounts of the experiences they have had of children not yet born. Children tell us about memories they have of events that are part of their lives and that happened before they were born.

Let these accounts speak for themselves. I have been wary about giving explanations. Meant as pointers, they were brought by the mothers themselves or arose in conversations. They are not intended to be scientific explanations. We have to emphasize that these dreams and symbols were experienced with great intensity as outstanding experiences.

If you approach these descriptions in an unbiased way, simply as accounts to begin with, they can lead to far-reaching questions. I should like to express the wish that new judgements are not immediately formed with the intention of their leading to 'better arguments', but that deep reflection may be stimulated in the reader about the mystery of the developing human being and about pre-natal existence altogether.

ANNUNCIATION

The messenger of God, in swirling mantle, came O so
    gently to my place of slumber
And, bending low to me, he said the words:
Be patient still for just a little longer, the boy is now
    already on his way! —

And like the sound of wind in velvet curtains, in one
    quick flash, the holding of a breath,
The silence broke, and lo! I heard it clearly, your
    footsteps, child, your footsteps coming, coming to me,
    from distant hills, from far away.

Ina Seidel

Some Accounts by Expectant Mothers

It is not such a rare event for expectant mothers to have a deep connection to their unborn child, or even to dream about it. They already know something of the child's appearance, its disposition or its destiny, although its body is still being formed within their womb and is not yet ready for birth.

Many of these premonitions are probably not taken too seriously or they are forgotten again, whereas other mothers take them so seriously that they do not want to talk to other people about them, which is perfectly understandable. Therefore we should be all the more grateful to those mothers who, often after initial hesitation, do speak out about their experiences. They appreciate that what such accounts can mean to a third person is more important than protecting their own privacy.

Mrs F. describes the difficulty of conveying such an experience. When we read her account we see how intimate the realm is into which we are entering, and with what heedfulness and respect we have to approach it.

Mrs F.: It was quite some effort to get down on paper what I have been asked to impart, because the written word is different from my feelings. When I noticed that I had conceived, I very soon felt a strong connection to the developing child—which I find difficult to describe. Perhaps I could call it a feeling of wonder and expectancy, such as you have when you are waiting to welcome a person whom you all of a sudden love, but who you already know well (from physical appearance?). During sleep I was particularly strongly connected with the coming child—though I cannot describe this. But it must have been because of this connection that, without stopping to think about it, I knew for certain whether the coming child was a girl or a boy, and its name came to me, but I do not know where from.

Mrs B.: When I had been expecting my daughter for five months I had a dream in the night which made a strong impression on me. I saw the face of an embryo with large, wide-open eyes. A very delicate down was growing on its head and on the skin of its little face. It looked at me with an infinitely profound look, full of peace. It was almost smiling, and without moving its lips I felt it speaking to me. It gave me to understand that it was looking forward to coming to me, to being born and to lie in my arms. This unborn child looked at me for a long time, and its eyes were full of love. Then it turned its head away from me, and I realized that it was tired, and I should not disturb it any longer.

This dream was so alive and impressive that I shall never forget it.

When my daughter had been born and was a few days old lying in my arms, she opened her eyes and looked at me, and it was the same look, the same eyes which had looked at me in my dream. Infinitely profound, wise eyes. For a moment I had the same experience as I had had in my dream.

Mrs R.: In the seventh month of my first pregnancy I dreamt about the birth. Just the outer trappings of it: doctors in white overalls, a sturdy woman, the midwife, neon light, and me lying there. It was the hospital. Then a small, blond, blue-eyed boy came running towards me, took my hand and said: 'Well, here I am!' I had known his name for a long time. It had been with me since the third month.

Today he is one year and seven months old, and he looks exactly like he did in my dream.

Mrs D.: The first dream I had in this connection referred to my second daughter. When my first daughter had hardly been born I dreamt that I was standing on the stairs in the schoolhouse in H. watching my two daughters who were running hand in hand off to play. They were about four and five years old, had short dark hair, as they do indeed have today, and I also remember very well the shape of their heads. This is actually the strongest memory I have of the dream — their heads — as I only saw them from behind. They were wearing summer frocks, and in this dream I was very proud and happy about my sweet daughters.

As these things had not yet happened at that time, I did not read anything into the dream, especially as I would never have believed that my second child would also be a girl.

More from Mrs D.: The second dream was about my son. I dreamt I was lying in bed one night when I suddenly felt something underneath me. I reached down and took hold of a small boy. He was so tiny, and somehow did not have any fully developed limbs either. I just do not know how to explain it. He was like a wooden doll and the size of a pencil. No, that was not it. Now I know the expression: he was a Tom Thumb! My son was as long and as round as roughly two thumbs, one on top of the other, and he had the shape of a thumb and the corresponding lack of contours. I saw no sign of gender, yet he was a boy. The next morning I showed him off proudly, but people just laughed at me. Yet I was happy that I, too, had a son.

Right from the beginning the dream had set me apart, at the birth itself and with regard to the state of my feelings. My son was indeed smaller than average, and stayed that way for a long time, his growth being extremely slow.

Clearly these are all prophetic dream experiences relating to unborn children. In the second account we are given a particular aspect appertaining to the soul condition of the child developing in its mother's womb. It is filled with trust in the world, it is looking forward joyfully to being born — it is bound to its mother by deepest love. The dream pictures in the third to the fifth accounts describe events which will not become reality until several years into the future. Along with being told what the child looks like, mothers are also told something about the child's disposition. We are constantly being given in symbolic form statements about the children's character. The next account given by an expectant mother is an example of this, and at the same time we are brought more closely into the family situation.

Mrs L.: After the birth of my first child all kinds of duties involved me much more in external life, and this was no doubt why I was not consciously aware of some of the premonitions occurring during my second pregnancy. But I do know that at some point, probably in the first weeks of pregnancy, the idea occurred to me that my eldest son was a little lonely, and this led to me asking myself: why do we actually not have a second child? Until then we had thought of ourselves solely as a one child family, expecting this to remain so.

Throughout the whole pregnancy my mood was largely cheerful and confident. During the last months I dreamt about a wonderful horse as white as a cloud, which I saw galloping with great force. A long while before our son was born we knew what his name would be. I do not know exactly when I became aware of this, but I never doubted that it was the right name.

Our son was born a few days before the scheduled date. Throughout the whole day of his birth the mood of cheerfulness and confidence never left me. He was the smallest of our children, with the lowest birth weight. Looking at the delicate baby he was then, who would have guessed that he would soon grow sturdier and stronger than his brother, who, by the way, received him as a long-awaited companion. Before this he had been a restless sleepwalker, but from the moment of his brother's arrival he slept the whole night through.

I often think of the dream picture of the horse, for our son is full of energy, often showing a violent temperament, and full of warmth both in feeling and physically.

Dream images

Our dream world is frequently only the after-effects of our daytime experiences. However, it is not an unusual thing for the images of our waking life to take on an altered meaning through which they assume the character of symbols. Even outer stimuli reaching us in sleep can be turned into pictures by the dream. Everybody will probably have experienced a dream in which the bedcovers are too warm and they dream of a hot stove. Or a book drops to the floor and in the course of the dream they hear the sound of a shot, and so on.

But even pictures of events long past and often forgotten can flash up again in a dream and acquire a different character. For instance, problems worrying us at the present moment can appear as exam fever from our faraway school days.

The dream obviously makes free use of our store of

memories and links them in quite different, frequently very unexpected ways. As parables, they draw our attention to deep-seated, often quite unconscious processes within us.

In the previous description the coming child's disposition is presented in the image of a galloping white horse. In many of the following accounts too, situations and objects become symbols or, to put it better, the essence of the matter — water, clouds, flowers, colours, a throne, the interior of a church, and so on. The significance is usually no problem for those directly concerned, or it becomes obvious at a later date.

Experiences while awake

Expectant mothers can receive messages about their coming child not only in dreams but whilst in a particular frame of mind during the waking hours too. These do not necessarily occur at outstanding times, but particularly often in perfectly ordinary moments of daily life. Yet the inner awareness of the perceiver becomes so different that images referring to the coming child momentarily light up in them.

Mrs P.: My third and fourth children announced themselves in the following way. I was laying the table and my two big children were already sitting at the table when all of a sudden a third child was sitting there. For just a moment I saw it quite clearly. Then there was the occasion when I was at the playground after my family had grown to three. Suddenly I saw the third child, who in fact was still in the pram, now bigger, running round with the others, followed by a fourth, who looked fairly similar to the third.

On neither occasion was it a dream but like a quick flash in broad daylight. I cannot say exactly when this was, but it could have been about half a year before the fourth child was conceived.

Mrs G.: I had vivid experiences of my three children before they were born.

I had very close contact, prenatally, with my first two children. I knew very early on, in both cases, their names and their gender. Both names proved to suit very well both their character and their destiny.

When these two children were one and a quarter and two and a half, it happened that I was sitting with them at the edge of a wood in front of a slope. It was spring, and suddenly a tractor appeared, shattering the beautiful day's peace. All three of us were shocked by the unexpected noise. Then I felt a being approaching us from the wood on the other side, and I knew I would become pregnant again. It was as though I were receiving an annunciation.

A few weeks later I was out walking again with my two small children, and in the middle of the suburb we passed a large rubbish dump which had formed in a large bomb crater. I do not think refuse was actually being collected there. As we were going round it to reach a nicer area I heard a voice telling me the name of my child.

Mrs R.: In the third month of my second pregnancy I suddenly awoke in the night and looked over at my husband. On top of him lay a baby, large and round, with its eyes open, and a nose like its grandfather. I shut my eyes quickly in fright, and did not dare open them again.

From the seventh month onwards my opinion was that it was going to be a girl. But three days before it was born, as I was getting up in the morning a name occurred to me, and I thought how lovely it sounded. And B. did in fact come to us, seven days later than expected.

These last accounts show a common element. What is perceived does not correspond to the outer reality of the moment, yet it is felt with great intensity. The prediction is made with great force and prophetic significance, so that these occasions will remain forever in memory. It is a matter of spontaneous perception, the abrupt arrival of impressive images, which do not belong in the everyday course of events.

These prophetic dreams have the same character as messages received in the wakeful superconscious state: they are prophetic statements referring to destiny, the significance of which is already realized during the dream, and which has a durability which will forever remain in the memory. In this respect the difference between dream and waking experiences is of no importance. In both instances perception relates to a content which does not belong to the world of sense experience.

Such experiences appear to be becoming more and more frequent, as though the world of unborn souls is trying to enter more and more strongly into human consciousness. They are trying to wake us up and make us aware of our responsibility for coming generations and the continuation of humankind.

Desire and dream

It is essential to refer to the fact that it is possible that the dreamer's life of desire can play a part in a prophetic prediction. In the following instances a strong egoistic desire may have contributed to falsifying this prophetic dream.

A young woman, herself the third of four sisters, was already the mother of two daughters, and also aunt to several nieces. Half a year before the conception of her third child she dreamt about twins, a pair of boys, and in three dreams she saw them as sportsmanlike infants, as schoolboys and as young men. She eventually gave birth to identical twins, two sturdy girls.

The predictions in the case of Mrs E. were similar; she already had two sons and must have wanted a girl. In the fourth month she dreamt that she saw a girl of about twelve, tall and robust with thick blond plaits, standing in the half-open door, and she called her by name: 'Amethyst'.

Mrs E.: But it turned out to be a boy. He is now twelve years old and, in contrast to his four dark-haired brothers, he is tall, strong and blond. He does not speak much, keeps himself to himself, and has an upright, almost distinguished character. Amethyst means resistant to getting in a frenzy. At his christening we gave him this unusual name as a third name.

The dream picture of the child coincided in all its details with reality, and the mother experienced the child's character in accordance with the feeling content of the words and pictures of the dream. The name gives no indication of sex. The mother's personal wish, however, superimposed itself on the events in the dream and changed the boy into a girl.

The anthropological aspect

Artistically gifted mothers sent us portraits of their newborn babies and infants which they had painted during their pregnancy, and they always assured us that that was what their baby looked like at birth or as a toddler. Other mothers described the dream visions they had had during their pregnancy. In these they saw the children who had not been born yet either as youngsters or as adults. And this raises the question as to what extent a dream picture actually possesses the power to predict a person's character and personality.

How do we actually get to know a person? How do we come to experience something of his being?

When in ordinary life we meet people for the first time we first of all take in their outer appearance in a kind of picture: the face, the hair, the shape of the hands, the overall composition of the shape of the body — and this makes a strong impression on us. This goes further if they move or speak to us. Their words convey a world of thought and feeling. These signify their inner life, and in them lives their consciousness of themselves.

In our position as observer we also perceive the intonation and the volume of their voices, their manner of speaking, their gestures and mimicry, their walk, in fact we are actually perceiving their will impulses which remain largely hidden where they themselves are concerned. In a certain respect we can therefore say that when we meet people for the first time we get to know them better than they know themselves. Just notice objectively how spontaneously we form a judgement of the people we meet, and how often, after a long period of getting to know them better, this judgement is confirmed, and yet how far removed we usually are from judging ourselves correctly.

Even deeper layers of people's character are mirrored in their actions, especially in the way they work. And yet everything we can perceive in this way is related to their being as an image is to reality.

If we get the opportunity to follow a further stretch of people's biographies, we discover something of their path of destiny. As parents who are privileged to accompany their children for part of their way, we have wonderful opportunities to observe them. If we have several children, we can be amazed to see what a tremendous difference there is between their abilities and talents and the diversity of their paths of life. By the time they are grown up one would hardly guess from their individual differences that they had a similar start in life.

When an awaited child makes itself known to the expectant mother in a dream picture the mother is in a similar situation to us when we are meeting someone for the first time. She experiences something of the appearance of the coming child, whereby the gaze and area around the eyes, or the form of the head or the stature may be particularly emphasized. The image shows her the way the child walks and speaks, either as a toddler or as an older child. And the mother gets to know something about the character and the being of her child before it makes its appearance here on earth.

Seeing a person again after years or decades whom we knew well in their earlier years can give us special insight into people's capacity to change. The change may be so radical that we have difficulty in believing it is the same person. We may have to make a close examination of the features we once knew so well before we recognize our former friend.

In following up their path of development we are led to the thought that although a person's innermost being is actively engaged in developing and passing through change, yet it is the person himself who determines the changes that come about. The idea of an eternal core of being, a person's actual individuality, presses itself upon us. We can discern something of this when we look people in the eye, yet their innermost being remains to a large extent a deep secret.

Presentiments prior to pregnancy

In the accounts given here most of the pictures described could never have come from the child growing in its mother's womb, as the bodily forms and other means of expression are not yet developed. Therefore the child's *being*, from whom the form-giving forces obviously issue, has to be thought of independently of the body which is still in the process of coming into existence.

When we include the following accounts, then this independence from its bodily nature of the human being that is coming into existence will become clearer still. The first two dreams were experienced before even the beginnings of the children's bodily foundations existed. In the fourth account the whole series of future siblings is actually experienced after the birth of the first child.

Mrs W.: A while before I was pregnant I dreamt that in my arms lay a very small child who smiled at me and whose eyes shone as only those of very young babies can. It was a totally heavenly experience, and I was filled with a kind of bliss I had never experienced before. A strong love also went out from me to the child, and I knew the child was mine. I had no recollection of giving birth to it, but (in the dream) my mother assured me it had been born on May 10.

Another dream during this pregnancy was of encountering a three-year-old child in a playground. As in the first dream there was a heavenly feel about it, and the child gave me a radiant smile. I had a similar feeling of bliss and love for the child. I played with the child all day, and although it did not seem to have any parents, it was not mine. When evening came I offered it my hand, wanting to take it along with me. It smiled at me and said, 'Not yet,' in a very friendly manner, but definitely as a grown-up would; upon which I felt something like shame that I had expected or hoped to be able to take it with me.

Mrs F.: Six months before conception I dreamt that a child came up to me bringing two grown-ups with it, and said: 'These are my godparents.' The child disappeared in the dream, but the two godparents remained, and were clearly recognizable.

Mrs T. dreamt, before she conceived, that a son of about 18 spoke to her in a state of great excitement about important matters. He also gave her his name. But when she woke up she could neither remember what he spoke about nor what his name was. Yet she clearly retained an image of what he looked like which she recognized in the son to whom she actually gave birth.

Mrs G.: When my son was about four or five months old I had a strange dream one night. I was looking through the window out over our garden. High up in the sky I saw a lot of 'flying objects', large, bright and almost transparent, similar to the folded paper flyers the children make for themselves. Slowly they hovered up and down and to and fro, and in the background was the blue sky. This continued for quite a while and was then followed by quite a different picture. I was holding my son by the hand, who could already walk in the dream, and we were dressed in white. We were both radiantly happy as, smiling, we walked towards a gateway. Yet it was no ordinary walking, for with every step we were lifted high off the ground, and each step took us a long way forward. But it all proceeded slowly and lightly. The ground was soft and white, and the gate a round arch, light grey and almost transparent. We laughed together as we stepped through the gateway. On the other side everything too was white, and from both sides we were welcomed by happy, smiling people. Were they humans or other beings? They were also all dressed in white, and they too were very beautiful. They formed a pathway, and we returned their greeting and proceeded hand in hand, and everything was bright and light.

Far away in the distance there was seated in the middle of the pathway a small figure who was also dressed in white, and had either golden hair or a golden crown on his head. It was so far away that it was difficult to see what it was. This small figure was our Jules, and we walked on towards him, being greeted from both sides with radiant smiles to which we smilingly responded — and all was white, bright and light.

About a month later I became pregnant.

Mr C.: It must have been in November or December when I rounded off a busy working day in Berlin with a recuperative walk through quiet night-time streets under a clear, star-studded sky. Suddenly I felt a strong presentiment that from out of the cosmic expanses, of which the starry sky is the outer image in the sense world, the being of a child was on its way to me. This was all the more remarkable seeing that at this particular time there was no sign of my marrying in the foreseeable future. I had no means of knowing that my future wife had come from her homeland to Germany a few months before this. She was living and working for the time being in what had been my home town for the greater part of my life up till then. However, as my path of life had meantime taken me away from this town, destiny had some more 'adjusting' to do. My wife was transferred to M. and my work had arrived at a stage which required my return to M. At our very first meeting, which occurred outside the framework of our work, we experienced a strong feeling of belonging together. This was a few days before my wife started work in her new position. What a happy surprise it was for the both of us that the administration had picked the very department for her in which I worked!

Our daughter is now 16 years old. She has had the good fortune to see quite a bit of the world including several capital cities and her mother's enchantingly beautiful home town. In 1980 I decided it was time to take my family to see Berlin. As soon as we arrived I was amazed to see our daughter enjoying every moment with a kind of enjoyment I had never witnessed in her before. She confessed that nowhere else had she felt as happy as she did in Berlin, and that even walking along side streets was a delight to her! When, after this first visit there, holiday time came round once more she asked me whether we could spend it in Berlin again. We have let her do this twice more since then, and the desire to go there is still very much alive! This makes me wonder whether this is not connected with the fact that my child and I came into touch with one another for the first time just on this particular spot on earth.

Mrs B.: At the beginning of my first pregnancy I began on a book, a diary, in which I wrote down all the observations, thoughts and feelings I had during the time I was expecting. On the first page I did a little drawing with coloured chalks of a girl and a boy, as I then pictured my children. I am not good at drawing, and the result is certainly no work of art. But after both my children had been born, it struck me afterwards that in the picture the girl is larger and older than the boy, more delicately built and very blond. The boy is smaller and rounder, with sturdy arms and legs. And that is exactly how it turned out to be. Our daughter is one and a half years older than our son, delicate and quiet, whilst he is round, strong and very temperamental and energetic.

Mrs I. dreamt after the birth of her first child: I am taking Andreas [the first child] with me, and we are going out. There are two smaller children in the pram, and a very small one under a blanket which we can disregard.

Mrs I. had two more healthy children. With the fourth pregnancy she had to have a Caesarean section prematurely and the child died a few hours afterwards with dyspnoea syndrome (breathlessness).

An elderly lady, who had had a lot of children and grandchildren herself, told us among other things that her own mother said that around the time of each of her pregnancies she became aware of all the future siblings.

I would also like to draw attention to the well-known painting by Michelangelo *The Creation of Adam* where Eve and her children are already depicted there in the large cloak of the Creator God.

The last three stories show, in addition, a motif that will be frequently occurring in what follows, namely, the connectedness of siblings. They are obviously already connected in the prenatal world.

If you look at the series of siblings in various families you will observe certain laws. The position a child has in the family has a marked effect on the developing personality. In childhood and youth basic qualities of character are laid down which have a determining influence still in later life.

The examples given here show that it is no mere chance whether a child is the first, second or third child in a row of siblings, but that they so to speak 'agreed' to this beforehand.

The name is given

When a child is expected in a family, as the time of birth approaches thought is given to what the child's name should be. We skim through books, weigh up the favourite names of each of the parents, discard them, and then take a fresh look at them. If he is a boy he will be called 'Christian' and if it is a girl let us call her 'Anne'.

Just think how strongly we were shaped by our name, particularly during our childhood. By calling us by our name people are calling us to ourselves. As we get older the significance of the name decreases. We have found our identity and are not so much in need any more of confirmation from outside.

So when we realize that the name is something that helps to form the personality, it brings home to us what a responsibility we carry when we decide what our child's name shall be.

Therefore it need not surprise us when the beings who guide the incarnating soul from the spiritual world into our earthly world in some cases give the child a name and tell the parents what it is.

In this respect we have to ask the reader to show understanding with regard to the fact that the full name cannot always be given, or in some cases was changed. These reports, which will be passed on to a wider readership must, due to their delicate nature, remain anonymous, and the people who gave them to us also feel this way.

Let us start with examples describing how expectant mothers receive the name of their coming child.

Mrs H.: With our oldest child I dreamt in about the fourth or fifth month of pregnancy that I was sitting in a cellar, in a dark, restricted space, anxious and alone. A passageway led to the cellar, and the figure of a woman came towards me. She wore a large blue cloak, and a wonderful air of trust and confidence streamed out from her as she approached — a bit like the Virgin Mary. She was surrounded by light . . . and from all round her there sounded forth loudly from her to me the name 'Ursula'.

This dream was tremendously impressive, and I was sure I was going to have a girl. I felt that the dream was enveloping me in the being of the child to come.

Mrs H. did indeed have a girl.

Mrs H.: My fifth pregnancy, despite my being considerably unwell, was a raptuously happy time. It was again about the fourth or fifth month that I received the name in my sleep like a bolt from the blue. I loved the sound of it and thought I would have no difficulty in discovering what it meant. I was sure I would have a girl, and I accepted the name with a happy heart.

A healthy, chubby girl is now lying in her cradle, rejoiced over by her siblings and admired and loved rapturously by her parents.

Mrs X. told us that prior to the conception she perceived a bright light that kept circling round her, and from it sounded forth the words: 'My name is Angelika.'

Mrs J., who already had three children, wanted to have one more. But it did not come until later on, when Mrs J. actually felt too old for it. She writes and tells her now 14-year-old daughter: 'You are the only one of my children whose name I was privileged to "hear" in a dream, and quite clearly with C: Constanze. It was granted me to be given your name and also to see you in the dream, with brown eyes and brown, curly hair. I have to admit how like the dream picture you have become.'

Mrs K.: I had our sixth child when I was nearly 46. It must have been quite a while before the conception that I saw in an extremely poignant dream a boy of about five years old and heard the name 'Dominic'. (It was somehow more vivid than hearing.) My last child was about seven or eight years old. I was already going through the menopause. After five children (and other circumstances) we had not wanted to have another child. However, despite the fact that I did not wholly believe in this dream—I did not at that time know of anthroposophy—it must nevertheless deep-down have prepared me for it. I thought along the lines that although it was pretty unlikely, if it was the will of God, then I must at least leave my calendar out of the picture. But on the surface I must have come to the point of not thinking about it any more, so that it was not until I was in the fifth month that I noticed I was pregnant, as my monthly cycle had in any case already become irregular. Even I myself can hardly imagine how I managed never-theless to occupy myself intensely with choosing a name and yet telling no one about my dream. The whole matter must have seemed weird to me. When the child arrived, looking just as he did in the dream, I knew without doubt that he could have no other name than Dominic! When he was five he looked exactly as he had in the dream, and even today I can recognize the same form and features.

Mrs W.: On my way to work I could, on frosty mornings, see the red-gold sun rising along parts of my way, when it was not hidden behind rooftops. This moved me so much that, in a way I cannot understand at all, I began to pray to the sun for happiness and good fortune for my unborn child.

Perhaps it is important to say that having been born in 1933, and conceived and brought up according to the ideals of the Third Reich, Christianity was totally unknown to me.

As time advanced, I thought of the name Karl Richard for the coming child. The first name was after his grandfather, my father who had fallen in Finland, and the second name was after his father. It was at the end of June that one night I looked, in my dream, into a sky that was a moving white sea of gathering clouds, immense and powerful. High above me in the clouds there stood a wooden chair, tall and broad, with strong arm rests. A voice came forth from it, moving round in circles, until the whole cloud-filled sky was filled by it. It was similar to when a stone falls into the water and small and then ever larger circles spread out far over the water. The voice said: 'When you have a son call him Halyan.' Then the encircling voice grew quiet and faded away, the clouds disappeared and I fell again into an ordinary sleep. In September my first child, a son, was born.

Mrs E.: Our second son acquired his name in the following way. In my dream I wanted to call him Daniel, but a powerful voice coming forth from dark clouds said quite clearly: 'Not Daniel, David.' And that is what he was christened.

The name is brought to the mother in tremendously impressive pictures. We have a direct experience of the images coming to us from a world of a higher order than ours. The figure of the noble woman, the tremendous pictures of clouds, the experience of bright light and the resounding voice intoning the name make a huge impression on the people who witness them. And the name is accepted without question. We are reminded of the great archetype of such a happening, namely, the Archangel Gabriel's annunciation of the birth of Jesus to Mary, as described in the Gospel of St Luke, chapter 1, verses 30ff.:

And the angel said unto her, Fear not, Mary, for thou hast found favour with God.

And behold, thou shalt conceive in thy womb, and bring
forth a son, and shall call his name Jesus.
He shall be great, and shall be called the Son of the
Highest.

However, the following accounts in which the father
hears the name also have exalted archetypes. For instance,
we read in St Luke's Gospel, chapter 1, verses 11ff., that
while the priest Zacharias is serving in the temple an angel
foretells to him the birth of John the Baptist.

And there appeared unto him an angel of the Lord
standing on the right side of the altar of incense.
And when Zacharias saw him he was troubled, and fear
fell upon him.
But the angel said unto him, Fear not, Zacharias, for thy
prayer is heard; and thy wife Elisabeth shall bear thee
a son, and thou shalt call his name John.

A few contemporary examples:

Mr S. dreamt in the fourth or fifth month of his wife's
pregnancy that he saw a group of several children standing
near him. The one closest to him came running to him, and
he heard an inner voice saying to him: 'This one is Natalie,
who will be coming to you.' His wife had a girl.

Mr B. dreamt during an afternoon nap that his wife would
have an 'Andrea'. His wife then had her first child, a girl,
and they called her Andrea.

Mr W., whilst his wife was pregnant with their first child,
dreamt that he saw all of their six children in their order of
birth, what they looked like and what their names were.
And he said: 'If we had a further child, I would not know
what to think!'

When their fourth child was on the way **Mr B.** heard the name 'Julian' in a dream, and they had a son.

Mrs B. already had four children, and she did not know at the time that she was pregnant again. One day, when her husband was present, she told him that she could not stand the smell that was just arising, to which her husband said quite spontaneously, without giving it a thought: 'Of course you can't, because our Anna Katherina is on the way.'

This was how they became aware of the name of the child who was already expected.

Experiencing conception

Mrs S.: I married in 1942. While having intercourse with my husband (because of the war the room was completely blacked out, so there was no question of light reflexes) there appeared to our left, perceptible only to me, a cloud of light, and looking out of this cloud was a face without contours. Whereupon I told my husband: 'We are to have a son.' He did not doubt this for one moment, despite being unaware of the cloud of light.

During the war we often did not get enough to eat. So the following week I went to our family doctor asking for a pregnancy test so that I could get coupons for extra food. He asked me how long I thought I had been pregnant, and I said: 'Almost a week.' He laughed, and said we should wait a bit longer. I begged so hard that he gave me the test. And when I went back for the result he looked at me thoughtfully for quite a while, and said: 'You were right.' The face I had seen was there when the child was a baby, again when he was a boy, and I can see it now that he is a man. I could easily imagine it still being there when he is an old man. The boy was born in Berlin in 1943.

So Mrs S. knows, while intercourse is taking place, that conception is occurring, and at the same time she has the amazing experience of the cloud of light and the presence of the being of the child. In the examples to come a momentary glimpse of a difficult destiny is experienced or the descent of a form of light coming from infinite spaces and being transformed into a child in its mother's arms.

We are brought to a new interpretation of the idea of 'conception' — or is this the original meaning of the word? It means the receiving of the child's being from heavenly worlds (German: *Empfaengnis*) and not only the receiving of the male seed or the fertilizing of the ovum. (In English 'conception' can apply both to a child and to a thought.)

A great many of the accounts given in this book are basically about this moment. If, however, both the physical conception and the receiving of the child's being are experienced at the same moment, this signifies the spiritual presence of the child's being. But let us leave it to the ladies themselves to speak from their own experience:

Mrs B.: We had planned to have Elias six months later, but he was in a great hurry to come into the world. When I became pregnant I was aware of it before my doctor confirmed the pregnancy a few weeks later. I knew that I had conceived the moment it happened, and I knew at once that it would be a boy.

During the whole pregnancy we spoke only of 'him', which had nothing at all to do with the fact that we had wished for a boy. We accepted it with the same feeling of certainty and of it being a foregone conclusion as we did when we spoke of 'her' when I was pregnant later on with my daughter.

A description given by a 20-year-old woman experiencing a pregnancy in which there is strong conflict between the mother and the unborn child:

I knew I would conceive a child—it was as though a great dark space was coming towards me. However, I did not want to avoid it but go to meet it. And then, after the conception, I experienced ease of mind and the feeling that I could bear all the misery and hard times with a strength that came from the child and not from myself.[1]

A woman dreams that she is looking up into a night sky that is infinite. Soon there appears a shining starlike globe descending to her rapidly in spiralling curves. She spreads out her arms to receive it, and all of a sudden the globe of light is transformed and a little child lies in her arms. A short while later the woman becomes pregnant.[2]

Mrs V.: My son was born in the middle of the Second World War and was very much wanted. That means he could have arrived a year earlier. During the night before or after the conception I dreamt of him in the following way: a sturdy and happy little fellow of three or four years old came tramping down a slope towards me. The experience was so clear that I marked in his date of birth in my calendar with a little star. The doctor gave me another date, with the result that we had to wait for ten days for his arrival! Not until later did I remember my dream and check my calendar. The birth date was the very day that fitted with the dream I had had of the conception. Throughout my son's third and fourth year I was constantly amazed at the way the dream and reality coincided.

Mrs A.: The announcing of my children: While I was having intercourse with my husband, that is, neither sleeping nor dreaming, I suddenly saw an image of a small pond on which a lot of ducks were swimming haphazardly, proper colourful wild ducks. All of a sudden several of them dived, that is, their heads went under the water and their tails in the air. Then, apart from two of them, all the others swam away. These two stayed in the same position as though they had caught something in their beaks, until the image disappeared. And straight away I knew — we are going to have twins! I immediately told my husband. And nine months later identical twins, girls, were born, of which sadly the larger of the two died (in my opinion the gynaecologist was to blame, because he would not listen to me). The image I experienced was so clear and definite, that right from the start I never doubted the fact of my pregnancy with the twins, and everything is still absolutely clear and vivid in my memory (I am now 72 years old).

The ducks can be seen to be a symbolic guise for the souls of the children waiting to be born. This connection becomes quite apparent in the further course of the narrative. Other mothers and fathers tell of their finding their child in a dream, where it is either playing with a number of other children, or where their child breaks away from a larger group of children and comes towards them. The following account tells us how the mother is actually pushed into getting pregnant by the being of the child. This opens up another perspective of 'family planning'.

Mrs W.: We were a happy family with our two small children. I was busy in my profession and with other activities outside the family, and at this particular time we were not thinking of a further child. Then for a few days I was overcome with an inner restlessness. It was quite clearly a feeling that a child wanted to come to us. I talked to my husband about it. He was also prepared to have the child. We performed the union in a conscious attitude of receiving the life that wanted to incarnate. It happened only once, towards the end of the menstruation cycle, at a time when conception is less likely to take place—I had a sensation of a tone resounding loudly, and I was totally open to what was coming. Nine months later it made its physical appearance: a very strong child with dark eyes, who could hold its own head up in the first few days, and looked out into its new world with wide-awake eyes.

Dream pictures in the third week of pregnancy

The last stories told of the experience of the moment of conception being overshadowed by the being for whom the act is taking place, and there now follow accounts of dreams experienced in the third week of pregnancy. This is an important moment in the course of pregnancy. Even superficially it is the beginning of the actual embryonic development, and from a more inward aspect it is the moment when the coming individual touches down (see p. 61).

Mrs A.: First of all, our five sons always came at a time which they had probably chosen themselves. They did not adapt themselves to the wishes of their parents who would have preferred every time to have waited another year before getting out the cradle. So during the first three to four weeks I never knew that I was in the family way. I am mentioning this because every time it was almost exactly at the end of the third week after conception that I had unusually powerful dreams such as I had never had at any other time. The children all announced themselves in quite different ways.

The first time, I dreamt that my husband and I, who had been married for only about six weeks, had been invited to a special celebration being held for my brother and his wife. We appeared to be in the large hall of a hotel. A voice called on my sister-in-law to say a prayer in front of all the invited guests for her child whom she was expecting (she was indeed expecting her first daughter, and was in about the fourth month). Without any hesitation she spoke the prayer on a slightly raised stand, with a lot of people listening, me among them. We heard a very beautiful prayer. When the speaker had finished, I was all of a sudden also called upon to say a prayer, as I was also expecting a child.

I wanted to collect myself and think about it, but however hard I tried I could not find any words. I felt miserable. Then I noticed that the ceiling of the hall rose up and disappeared. I stood alone, at the front beside the church's baptismal font, and the crowd of people were sitting in front of me in the pews. I was still searching in vain for words.

Then indescribably beautiful colours began to flow down from above. Music that nothing could equal began to sound forth, growing in strength until it was like thunder. And it formed itself into a voice. The words were spoken so powerfully that when we heard them all the people threw themselves in terror onto the ground with their faces touching the earth. What we heard was: 'It cometh from my heart. I am well pleased with him. It returneth to my heart.' Then I awoke.

When my first son was born he had two club feet. A plaster cast put one of them right. The other one was operated on the first time after nine months, the second time 17 years later. The childhood and youth of our eldest child was very much overshadowed by illness and several visits to hospital. I often feared that we would lose our firstborn. I always felt helpless in face of his destiny which was also difficult in other respects. He is 35 years old now, and today he is in good health.

With regard to my second son I can remember having two significant dreams, one of them again at the end of the third week—before I suspected I was pregnant—and the second a little later.

In the first one I was kneeling at the open window of my former nursery (in fact I was also sleeping there, as I was visiting my mother). I felt my husband standing behind me a little to the left. To begin with we were silent. I was holding up my arms and hands, and bathing them and my face in the damp coloured bubbles of a glorious rainbow, which reached down from the sky through the window onto (or into?) my body. I heard myself saying to my husband, in dialect, 'Can you see that?' and he answered, 'Yes, I can see it.' We did not see a child, but I felt it entering into me, and I can still remember well the blissful feeling engendered by the dampness and the play of colours.

Many years later I read a poem by Albert Steffen in which he describes the descent of unborn souls to earth. They come from heaven over the rainbow bridge.

As I awoke from the dream I knew for certain that I was pregnant.

In the case of the fifth child I was sitting among a lot of people dressed in black, on a chair in the row behind the others. Nobody looked round. They were all looking fixedly into the front right corner where someone was standing who, in their opinion, was about to be condemned. He does not live like they do. All of a sudden I saw him. He was wearing a snow white shirt, and had his back to us. He was a young man. I suddenly knew that he was my son, and that he was innocent. Then I awoke. It soon became evident that I was pregnant.

Water dreams

Mothers tell us again and again that during pregnancy they dream about water. This kind of dream is often the first indication of the beginning of pregnancy. They experience water in strong, flowing movement, or themselves swimming in foaming waves of a raging sea or calm, transparent water, clear springs and many other forms. These are indications of the radical changes going on in the mother's life organism. Water is after all an element that penetrates everything else and can adapt to any form. Its flowing movement shows very complicated forms that comply with laws belonging to the realm of life, and wherever life appears it is accompanied by the flow of fluid.

So water, the fluid element, can be the basis of life, and therefore it is not surprising if the beginning of a new life coming into being with the help of the mother's life organism is symbolized in her dreams in the form of water.

Two representative examples out of many:

Mrs E.: I am swimming all alone in a very wide, very murky river and am at the mercy of huge waves lifting me up high and then letting me fall again. A second river is entering from the right making strong eddies. A storm is threatening and I am very afraid. But I know that I must not give in now, that it is vital that I have to go on swimming.

Mrs B.: The sun is shining on a weir — this is like a little wall, cordoning off the small river, but diagonally, so that the water flows gently over it. It is covered with soft moss so that the water splashing over the ridge is very flat. I am sitting in the sparkling, sun-warmed water on the weir in the moss, feeling the water running warm and golden over my hands and legs. And I feel as happy as a child.

Flower dreams

It is not only water that plays a role in the following dream descriptions but the flower world appears at the same time. Plant nature is pure life on earth, with no will of its own, no soul life of its own that wants to express itself, but is attached to the earth environment, especially water, and is totally open to the sun which every year draws forth the plant world to new life. It is only in the blossom that we see an image of soul life, though this is of an entirely impersonal kind, shared by them all, and is totally unegoistic, wanting nothing for itself. This is why we human beings have such a particularly close attachment to flowers, because they present us with an image of pure soul life. When we want to give pleasure to people we give them flowers, because this expresses our feeling of inner connectedness. So we are not surprised if the descending child souls are announced by flowers, as the following examples show.

Mrs N.: In my second pregnancy I dream that I am walking along a pretty lane until I come to a small bridge. In front is a large meadow, to the left is the edge of a dark pine wood, and to my right a babbling brook. The meadow is a fresh, full green, and is covered with short-stemmed blossoms that look like daisies yet are as big as marguerites. I could stand gazing at the meadow for ever, and keep saying to myself: 'What a wonderful sight—this green meadow covered with white flowers with their golden-yellow centres!'—I was astonished at how white they were. How immaculate!

The reality that followed was that my son was always unusually content and helpful. He was also extraordinarily gifted—up till now we have found no subject he could not find some way of coping with, both bodily and practically as well as mentally and artistically. His exterior matches his inner being—I see him as an image of extraordinary harmony.

Mrs E.: Shortly after I conceived my fourth child I dreamt of flowers again. In a marshy ditch which I had to jump over and which was covered with all kinds of marsh grass, there was a golden-green brightness and an atmosphere of profuse, lavish, moist plant growth. On the other side of the slope, however, the earth was bare, damp and clayey. At the edge of this area there grew two lilies-of-the-valley, which were in full bud and just about to open.

Flowers are a particularly convincing symbol because we understand them altogether as an image of something higher. In these dreams (including the following ones) we see flowers with white blossoms (marguerites, anemones), representing in their purity a quality still untouched by contact with the earth. The lily family also belongs here (tulips and lily-of-the-valley). The whole group of plants related to the lily show in the whole way they grow that they are not very attached to the earth. We see this in the relatively slight way in which they take root, in the fact of their being bulbs which make them independent of their environment, and the very unformed leaves they have, and then the simple crown of the blossom which changes under our very eyes from green into the most beautiful shades of the petals.[3]

Artists of earlier ages knew this. They painted the angel Gabriel, announcing to Mary the birth of the Jesus Child, with a lily. The rose on the other hand is allotted, in Christmas pictures, to the child who has already come down to earth. The rose roots deeply in the earth, becomes woody, and only after several years does this wood give way to blossoms.

So these flower dreams are giving us a clear message. They are conveying that the being of the child comes to us not from the earthly world but from the realm of the heavens.

Children who cannot remain here

In what follows it is also flowers which tell the mother that the child is coming. The image of the fading of the flower already indicates that the children do not intend staying but will be returning to the world they come from. The parents' pain is in no way lessened by the memory of the dream, yet it can undergo transformation and bring them insight into the necessity of such an occurrence.

Mrs E.: In my sixth pregnancy I saw in my dream an area of forest in which there were anemones that were losing their leaves.

Our daughter was not capable of surviving and died a day after the emergency Caesarean operation.

Mrs E.: My first pregnancy began with a dream image (in the night following our union).

I saw a vaseful of tulips that were almost dead, and which hung limp out of the vase so that I could see into each withered corolla. The tulips were of various colours and stood on a desk beside the open window. A warm summer mood was in the air. (Mrs E. did not like tulips very much.)

I can remember a second dream during the same pregnancy. A large square willow basket had been prepared as a cradle. The child lay in it, but I could not see it. All I knew was that the cradle was not properly equipped. The mattress was too thin and I still had to fetch the coverlet from somewhere. It was obvious that the child was freezing and I should do something about it, but I was somehow being prevented from doing so.

At the end of the second month I had a miscarriage.

The last dream account—as well as the following examples—express the fact that the immediate environment is apparently not ready for the coming child. Strangely unmotherly feelings are described. We have to realize that on the one hand the most important content of the dream is the drama and the feelings this produces. The feelings are the reality, showing that the dreamer was aware of having to do something to help, but that she was somehow prevented. So the dream presents factually that she could not get herself to care for the child — perhaps was not meant to do so! We have to learn to regard our own feelings quite objectively as an observer.

Mrs D.: A very short pregnancy must have existed at some time in between, as the following dream shows.

I was assigned the job of supervising my sister's child and my child in the garden. They lay side by side in a baby basket. My sister's child — which was already there — had a strong round face. Beside it my child — which was not born yet — was delicate, small and dainty. It began to rain. Funnily enough I picked up my sister's child and took it indoors and left mine lying in the rain.

After that my period stopped for quite a while, but came again about four weeks later. I did not feel very well, and I was sure I had had a miscarriage.

Mrs W. told us the following dream. Her child was not dressed warmly enough. Whilst changing the baby she realized it was cold. Through carelessness the child fell off the table. In the dream she did not have much interest in the child.

She then has a miscarriage and reproaches herself for being so unready to receive the child.

Mrs A.: With my fourth child, once the pregnancy had been confirmed I waited in vain for a dream. I did not have one. Although I felt well for five months, soon after the end of the fourth month I had a shattering experience such as I had never had in my life before. While I was on my own doing my housework I was making the bed when I heard a voice speaking to me loudly and clearly in the Queen's English (not in my usual dialect): 'I am not coming onto this earth.' To start with I felt a great uneasiness which, however, gradually gave way to confidence. Even the doctor was surprised when in the fifth month the child was born dead.

Angelic beings

Up to now the stories have described phenomena of light, clouds and voices appearing in connection with an annunciation. These point to the presence of beings that are living in the surroundings of the unborn soul and accompanying the child on its way to birth. In the following accounts there is a clear perception of the angel that brings the being of the child and utters its name.

Mrs K. gave us this story:

In a village in the vicinity of B. there lived a country woman who often came for advice to my mother who worked in the area as a teacher. On one occasion she came along very agitated, saying: 'Madam, what would you say to this? I was at the priest's and I told him that I was expecting another baby and it would be a boy. To which the priest said that I could not possibly know that yet, as the child was not even there. So I told him that I had seen my little boy's angel and he had told me that my little boy should be called Max. The priest then said: 'My good lady, you are just imagining that, for angels are not the kind of thing we can see.' So I said: 'Your Reverend, you cannot say that, for I have always seen my children's angels, and they are not all the same. They all look slightly different, but all of them are beautiful. You, your Reverend, cannot have seen any angels.'

She then asked my mother what she would say to that. My mother calmed the woman down, and told her: 'Of course, if you say you see angels then I believe you, and you are a lucky person. But we cannot take it for granted that everybody can see angels.'[4]

I, however, who was a little girl then, would have been only too happy if I could have gone home with the woman to see the angels with her.

The three-year-old son of **Mr E.** told him his dream in the morning: An angel came with a child in his arms.

The father asked gently, 'Was it a boy or a girl?'

'It was a little girl,' the boy replied.

When the baby arrived it really was a girl.

Mrs I.: I have been looking after little Anne for two years. At a time when she gave the impression of being more or less transparent and was often sad, Anne dreamt the same dream several nights running.

An angel came to her who had a transparent star hovering over his head. It was very beautiful. The angel turned round and moved slowly ahead of her. Anne followed him further and further. They climbed a very high mountain; at the top it was all white, for it was covered with snow. Then the angel turned round and wanted to take her further, but at this point she woke up each time.

In earlier times it was taken for granted that people spoke about guardian angels, particularly to children. This happened not only out of tradition. This was fully justified because every now and then there were people who could see angels. At the present time humanity has lost the possibility of spiritual sight. This was a necessary development for only in this way could human beings become inwardly independent. Sense perception alone and the natural-scientific way of thinking that this leads to form the prerequisites for the attainment of freedom.

Only in exceptional circumstances do people see angels nowadays, for instance angel beings can confront a person with the fact of death. Stories of this kind are associated especially with the war years, when people hung in constant fear of death on the battlefield or during air attacks on cities.

In his lectures Rudolf Steiner describes angels as the guiding spirits of individual people. An angel leads us human beings into the earthly realm, accompanies us on our path of destiny, and then leads us through the gate of death, back into the world we came from.

The previous stories make it quite clear that these annunciations are about beings that already exist before conception and that want to incarnate on the earth. Nevertheless we face insoluable riddles to begin with if we consider individual people and their destiny.

How are we to understand the differences between children of one family, such as the varying dispositions and talents which determine their individual paths in life? Were these acquired in the world beyond, as gifts from the beings that guide us there? Many of our capacities have to be striven for by means of hard work and perseverance. For example, we learn as children to write. We go to great pains to master the art of using our hand properly, as we set down one letter beside another. In later life we have the capacity to write, but have forgotten all the tedious hours learning it in childhood.

Particular gifts that we have 'brought with us' often enable us to exercise a certain capacity with such unbelievable speed and agility as though we had been preparing to do this for a long time. When exactly was this preparatory work done? Certainly not in this lifetime, as was the case with writing. Did we do it then in a former life?

How are we to understand strokes of destiny, good or bad, which often radically alter a person's path in life? Can we not sometimes feel, especially if we survey a fairly long stretch of life, that these have their meaning and purpose well after the event? Do they not then seem to be balancing out something we have already lived through, but at a time lying prior to this life? We have encounters with other people, situations which seem to trigger memories, although they are happening in this life for the very first time. It occurs time and again that certain people have vague ideas or even clear memories of things that they experienced a long time ago and which come from well before the present earth life.

We shall now bring some things which children have said, and which point to repeated earth lives. Older people too can have presentiments of previous incarnations. It is evident that our 'forgetting' can on occasion be interrupted.

References to former earth lives

Mr. O.: It was springtime, and little Justina (three years old) was dancing up and down on her bed one afternoon during a thunderstorm. She was very excited, and also very happy. In childlike language, not grammatically perfect, she danced for joy as she came out with the following statements:

'I died once, and made this me!'

'I will die one day, but I shall make myself again!'

'When I die I will turn into a coloured butterfly, a little ball!'

'I lived before, and I had died.'

'You were looking for me, where your Niunia was.'

Mrs S.: When my little daughter was three years old she used three or four very strange words over and over again. Some while later a man from Israel came to our farm. When he heard the words he was able to tell us what they meant. They were very old Jewish names hardly met with any more in Israel today.

One particular situation I can remember very well. I asked my little girl whether she would come and help me bake. 'No!' she said, 'I am busy making mashke!' Towards evening I gently asked her again, and received the same answer. So I asked Simon the Israeli what mashke meant. It is an alcoholic drink that had that name about a hundred years ago. The word is not used any more today.

A single mother with a three-year-old son: 'Mummy, when I have grown up you will have become small again, won't you? And when you were little I was big, and because I am a boy I was your father. All we need is a mother...

'And being little, and because I am a boy, I asked you please to be my dear Mummy...'

Mrs C.: I got to know my nephew when he was barely four years old. Standing by the window, he liked showing me the houses his little friends lived in. He seemed especially fond of an old villa with small towers and balconies, which lay some distance away. When I asked him why he liked it so much, he said: 'You know, when I was still big I lived high up on a mountain, and the home I lived in had towers and windows like that.'

A boy of ten—let us call him Christopher—brought a school friend home with him, a girl. The two of them were playing together indoors. The boy's mother was sitting in an adjacent room with the door open. The girl came from a home where there is no religion at all and her schooling is also strictly atheistic. That day the teacher had been talking about landowners in the history lesson and had described them as exploiters and slave drivers. The children were playing at farms, with miniature houses and trees, wooden animals and farm workers. As they were playing the girl said casually: 'That was quite wrong what our teacher said today about landowners. It was absolutely different then, much nicer!' And she went on, with great enthusiasm, to talk about life on such a farm, what the house looked like inside, what the one and the other person did. And she spoke with particular interest about horses and riding, how wonderful it was to fly through the air like that, and many other things.

Then she said: 'You know, Christopher, I know exactly what it was like. I think I have done all the things that go on on a farm of that kind. I have been there before.'

And now comes an inspired picture of the process of reincarnation taken from standing in a queue in a crowded shop: 'I imagine this is how it happens with people. When we die we get to the back of the queue, and when we get to the front we come back to earth again!'

Mr W.: When I went to hear a lecture by a teacher I knew well I had a peculiar, unaccountable feeling as he stepped up onto the rostrum, so that on the way home after the lecture I gave some thought to what it could mean. I knew Rudolf Steiner's indications that a person gives expression to earlier incarnations in his gestures. But I could not find an explanation. During the night, however, I dreamt that in a bygone age I was standing on the forum in Rome and my friend was ascending the rostrum—clad this time in a Roman toga. When I awoke I saw at once that the movements of the speaker in my dream and those on the previous evening in the lecture hall were exactly the same. The evening speaker moved as though he were wearing a Roman toga, but because he had a present-day suit on I did not see it.

Mr S. gave us this story about his mother. Without any motivation whatsoever (i.e. for no apparent reason) his mother once heard a voice telling her that he and his father had been friends in former lives. Mrs S. was the daughter of a Protestant vicar, and had no knowledge at all of the concept of reincarnation.

It is possible to accept the idea of repeated earth lives simply as a hypothesis without, to start with, forming a judgement that either rejects or accepts it. Then look at life and at other people's destinies from this trial standpoint, and see what happens. All of a sudden totally new perspectives will open up when observing particularly difficult destinies, such as people who are either exceptionally beautiful or ugly, or people who are handicapped either physically or mentally—in fact when observing the state of being of anyone one meets. Many things that happen in life suddenly become explicit and acquire new, profound significance. The thought of repeated earth lives becomes a necessity.

However, for there to be the possibility for an individual to progress in his development it is necessary that the person learns lessons from his former lives and brings resolves into the following incarnation. A person's destiny, then, is the consequence of deeds and actions in his previous lives which have become resolves and intentions for this one. Human beings are given the freedom to shape their destiny, and in so doing work at the further development of the eternal core of their being. Rudolf Steiner tells us that many centuries elapse between death and a new birth. A human being fills this 'time span' by working through the experiences he had in his past life and preparing for his new life on earth.

What prevents us believing in earlier earth lives is chiefly the materialistic world conception which conditions us not to see the underlying depths in our existence, as well as the centuries-old tradition of the Christian confessions opposing and suppressing this idea. Yet if we read the New Testament attentively, we can discover clear indications in its favour.

At the beginning of chapter 9 of St John's Gospel we read: 'And as Jesus passed by, he saw a man which was blind from his birth. And his disciples asked him, saying: Master, who did sin, this man or his parents, that he is born blind?'

This question the disciples are asking Jesus contains the possibility that the blindness of the man born blind could be the result of his own deeds. This is therefore pointing to deeds which can only have happened before his present earth life.

In Matthew 11, verses 14 and 15, Jesus says of John the Baptist: 'And if ye will receive it, this is Elias, which was for to come. He that hath ears to hear, let him hear!'

This is a clear statement about the reincarnation of Elias in John the Baptist.

But the most important reason why we reject the idea of repeated earth lives is our forgetting of it. By and large we do not remember an earlier incarnation. But once we accept the idea of reincarnation, would the memory of former earth lives perhaps hinder us from making sufficient use of our present existence? There may be good reasons why memory is denied us, and that we time and again have to drink the draught of forgetfulness when we set out on a new earth journey.

In his *Education of the Human Race* Lessing says: 'You have so much to take with you along your eternal path! There are so many side steps!... So why could each individual human being not have been present in this world more than once?...

'Why could I not have already taken all the steps for my perfecting which a person can acquire purely from temporal punishments and rewards?

'And why not another time all those steps to which the prospect of everlasting reward gives us such tremendous encouragement?

'Why should I not come as often as I am capable of acquiring new knowledge and accomplishments?

'Do I gain so much on *one occasion* that it is not worth the trouble to come again?

'Is this why? — Or because I forget that I have been here before? But let me be glad that I forget it! The memory of my previous existence would allow me to make bad use of my present one. And what I *must* forget now, have I forgotten for ever? Or because so much time would be lost to me? — Lost? — What is there to lose?

'Is not the whole of eternity mine?'

The idea of repeated earth lives had its place in many of the representative cultural circles of the West over the last few centuries. We can certainly assume that this idea belongs to the Western heritage, even if it does not necessarily appear on the surface. We are in no way dependent on looking for it in Eastern religions. In Rudolf Steiner's anthroposophy it is founded anew from out of his own spiritual research, and made a focal point of a comprehensive conception of the world and of man.[3]

Life Between Death and a New Birth

It became clear from the previous descriptions that the human being is already in existence before conception. Let us begin with an account by a contemporary. In the case of Mrs Sch. the door which usually closes when we start a new journey on earth has not closed completely. She is able to describe memories from out of personal experience which show a connection between her past and her present earth life.

Mrs Sch.: I can remember very well the period after my death in my last incarnation. I saw a great panorama of my last life as though I was looking at it from a raised position—a kind of huge picture in which my whole past life was spread out before me. I had to pull myself away from it and hold firmly in my awareness to what I should take with me from it; the essential thing was this retaining of something.

After about three days—I still had an almost earthly feeling for time—this picture gradually disappeared, and I found this a very painful experience.

Then it was as though I was being thrown into a dark space and I was alone with my faults. I was at the mercy of my own imperfections, as though I were drowning in them, and it was very painful. And to start with there seemed no end in sight. It lasted a long time—I do not know how long—until very gradually I felt easier.

I now came together with a lot of other souls. There was a loving mingling with one another and then separating again, and it gave me great happiness to be with these people whom I particularly loved.

Later on I could help other people, such as people who

had died too early and found it difficult to adjust to their new environment.

I had an especially close relationship to my present father, and it was a tremendously painful experience when he left me to return to earth again, until he gave me the promise to remain connected with me and to continue to help me. Then everything went very quickly.

Now a kind of game began, to get down to earth. With the strong desire to acquire a body I time and again came into close contact with my father's seed. I was in a kind of struggle with a lot of other souls who also wanted to arrive on earth. It was a strong effort of will, but time and again it failed, and the game and the struggle to be the first began all over again. I found it more and more difficult and eventually had to give up. Then I all of a sudden suc-ceeded — though probably not due to me alone.

Then I can remember at the age of six weeks having recognized my father and smiling at him when he opened the curtain over my cradle and looked in.

In my childhood and youth I had a kind of clairvoyance. I could see what would happen in the future to those around me. Once when, on being questioned, I had prophesied a person's future, and given him a bad shock, I realized I should learn to curb this ability and transform it. This. however, means working on myself.

From among the many books and lectures of Rudolf Steiner in which he describes the life between death and a new birth I will select a few passages. I want to choose something that will help people extend their view beyond birth and beyond death, and bring together the 'where do we go to?' and 'where do we come from?'. For further reading there are anthoposophical books accessible to everybody today, especially the book *Theosophy*. (See the Bibliography, p. 228.)

There is a great reservation about giving detailed descriptions of a realm which has been unknown up to now. How can anyone give such reports about a world of which a 'normal' person has no perception? Rudolf Steiner pointed to the fact that the ability to look consciously into the spiritual world is potentially there in everyone, albeit in a dormant state. This ability has first of all to be developed. Rudolf Steiner has in many different ways and on many occasions described the path which leads today, in a modern way, to a development of these abilities, especially in his book *Knowledge of the Higher Worlds*. We soon discover that the prerequisites for unfolding these capacities are of a moral nature, and that there are barriers protecting human beings from entering unprepared into a world which can only be entered unharmed by souls that have prepared themselves for it.

There are descriptions of three stages of higher knowledge, and only the highest of these gives a person a clear view into these worlds. Steiner was able to make clear statements about these worlds. But all human beings who make use conscientiously of their natural human understanding can understand these accounts and apply them with insight so that many of life's problems can be solved, and they can have light thrown on many of life's mysteries, which helps them on their journey.

Human beings rank highest among the other three kingdoms of nature. Stones, plants and animals also have, as we do, a 'physical body'. At present, the physical body is all that we can perceive with our senses; also everything that surrounds us in nature that is apparently lifeless or dead—the mineral world in its solid, liquid and airy form—is of the same nature as our physical body. Yet there is a great difference between the human body and, for instance, a crystal. The latter retains its rigid form until it is either destroyed by being impinged on from outside or dissolved by chemical processes, whereas the human body has a 'champion who opposes disintegration'. This force that is active in all living beings is called by spiritual science the life body or ether body. It is also active in animals and plants.

The life body is the organizer within the living organism; it raises dead matter onto the level of higher laws, namely, those of the realm of life. Only at death does the life body separate from the physical body, and then the laws of disintegration enter again into the corpse in the form of physical and chemical processes.

Over and above the formative forces of life human beings have within them something that does not figure in plants but comes to expression otherwise only in the animal realm: feeling, everything to do with pleasure, pain and desire. Spiritual science calls the invisible bearer of emotions the sentient or astral body.

The fourth member of a human being is the one which raises human beings above the animal realm. Each human being is a unique being, an individual in himself. One can say 'I' only to oneself. Everything to do with species, which is the determining factor in animals, drops away when one is focusing on a particular human being, an individual.

So the members of the human being are:

physical body
life body (ether body)
sentient body (astral body)
ego

Only in the waking state do these four members interpenetrate one another. The resistance of the physical body awakens the ego to full consciousness. When we go to sleep the two higher members — the astral body and ego — leave the physical and etheric body to a certain extent. During sleep the astral body and ego connect with the soul and spirit world which surrounds us all the time. Under the direction of higher beings regenerative activity goes on within the physical and life body. However, as the ego does not have the resistance of the physical body, it does not know anything, on waking, of the events taking place at night. Only in dreams do we sometimes become aware, in a way that is beyond memory, of experiences we have undergone in the soul and spirit world.

Life after death

In sleeping and waking a human being's members alternate in a daily rhythm between separating and interpenetrating again, whereas at death the human members separate for good. When death has occurred the forces of disintegration set to work on the body at once. It is obvious that the 'champion who opposes disintegration' has withdrawn. The life body, sentient body and ego all leave the physical body.

The first experiences occurring after crossing over the threshold of death have been described by people who have been exposed to a tremendous shock. In recent years a number of books have appeared in which people who have been reanimated have told of their experiences. Owing to an accident or a life-threatening operation, they passed into an in-between state between life and death. In many cases they were diagnosed as being clinically dead but were brought back again with the help of doctors. They are all unanimous about seeing a huge review in which they had a survey of their whole life in a vast panorama. Everything they had experienced in their lifetime appears before them with incredible clarity and they also pass judgement on it, but with quite different criteria from the ones they used in their ordinary state of consciousness. It feels as though all this happens in seconds. But, as in a dream, time here has a different dimension.

In the course of life all our experiences are stamped on our life body as memories. When this is released from its function as a life force in the physical body human beings can oversee in these memories the whole of their past life.

Through spiritual-scientific research Rudolf Steiner has described how, in their life after death, human beings retain an extract of this vast memory tableau, which is not lost to them and which they take along with them. After a few days the life body, like a second corpse, slowly dissolves into the general life structure of the world, the universal cosmic ether.

This gives human beings a feeling of expanding, of becoming ever larger, and growing beyond themselves. They feel spread out over the things in their environment. Putting it abstractly: they no longer feel as though they are in the centre, as we do during earth life, but attached to the surrounding circumference. This circumference grows larger all the time in gigantic sphere-sized strides. We experience the spiritual spheres of our surrounding celestial bodies, first the moon, then the planets and the sun.

First of all human beings dwell in the soul world in the moon sphere. In our soul body all the desires generated in life are still active. However, the means to satisfy them are lacking, as that was only possible whilst living in a physical body of sense on earth. So there wells up in us a feeling of being deprived, like an all-consuming thirst. Greek mythology gives expression to this in the picture of the torments of Tantalus. The feeling of deprivation increases to a fiery heat in which souls are immersed. Purgatory and Gehenna are the terms applied to this in Christian and Islamic cultural circles. The Indians called this condition Kamaloka. Feelings of cold are also experienced, connected with things people neglected to do on earth. Human beings must learn here to free themselves from the attachment to the life that is over. They have to create new organs for themselves to be able to live in the soul world.

Human beings, as soul-spirit beings, now begin to travel backwards through their earthly lives from the moment of death until their birth. However, this time we do not feel ourselves to be the active agents of our deeds, for it is now a case of experiencing the effects we had on others. If, for instance, we have done something bad to another person we now have to feel the suffering we caused him. Alongside this we also judge our past deeds. We cannot do anything else but judge the value of our past life morally. And we prepare ourselves a 'package' consisting of these moral evaluations which we leave behind in this sphere as we move on along our after-death journey. This condition of Kamaloka lasts about as long as the time we spent sleeping, about a third of our lifetime.

When we have followed through our past earth-life back to our birth, suffering the effects of our deeds, we can then leave behind us a third corpse, the part of our soul body which contains our desire and passion nature, and this can now also dissolve.

Human beings are now ready for the spirit world, which in Christian circles is called the kingdom of heaven. This is the meaning of Christ's words to his disciples: 'Verily I say unto you: unless you become as little children you shall in no wise enter the kingdom of heaven.'

When, as purified souls, we can leave the region of burning passion (Kamaloka) and ascend to the further regions, we now associate with those people we were close to in life. But in the first instance these soul relationships present themselves as unalterable from the form they had in life. Homer spoke in this connection of 'the realm of the shades' where no change, no alteration is possible.

On the further path through the soul and spirit world

souls are constantly having to face their mistakes and shortcomings until there arises the strong will to change ourselves, which is only possible, however, in a new life on earth. Out of this will to compensate for our errors, to develop further and to make ourselves more whole the wish arises to enter again into life on earth.

In the spirit sphere of the sun into which we now come we human beings associate with people of all nations, races and religions. But this phase can only be entered into consciously if, during earthly life, we have acquired an understanding for all peoples. Here in the spirit sphere of the sun we encounter the being of the Christ who accomplished his deed of salvation for people of every race and religion, so that humankind can become united not in fanaticism but in universal understanding. Christ can only become the guide of human beings if we human beings endeavoured to form an inner connection with the Christ Being in the course of our past life. Christ provides us with light for our further path through spiritland.

Preparing for the new life on earth

Human beings now begin, under the guidance of the highest of spiritual beings, to work at the archetypal image of their coming life on earth. This creative activity brings us the greatest bliss. No earthly activity which makes us happy can be compared to this heavenly activity, and it fills us with the greatest feelings of happiness. As we proceed, the forces of the whole of the cosmos are woven into this archetypal image. Engaged in this activity are the highest of the spiritual beings (called by Christian tradition thrones, cherubim and seraphim), the external image of their activity being the zodiac in our starry world. They proffer certain gifts necessary for the construction of the archetypal image of the physical body, and which also signify particular inclinations in the coming life on earth. Our capacity to be receptive depends on our stage of development and what we have achieved in our past earthly life.

In some fairy tales, which are basically a description of life between death and a new birth, the 'gifts' are referred to in picture form. Let us remember for example the industrious girl and the lazy girl in Mother Holle, who are given gold or pitch as they return through the 'gate' to earth.

Preparation has to be made for the descent of the human being into the earthly world. The beings of the spiritual hierarchies withdraw more into the background again. There now arises a stronger feeling of the self in the descending human being, and an interest begins to awaken for actual earth conditions, for human history and for certain earthly human beings. As spiritual beings we take an interest in particular generation sequences at the end of which will be the couple we have chosen. We are especially attentive to the presence of certain tendencies and abilities in our future row of ancestors. Under the guidance of spiritual beings we take part in the planting of certain abilities, which, through the stream of heredity, will eventually be part of our make-up. Of special importance to us is the meeting of our parents, which is the prerequisite for our birth on earth. So we can say that on their way to incarnation human beings certainly have an influence on bringing their father and mother together.

As we make our way towards birth we now return from spiritual worlds into the soul world, passing once more through the spheres of the planets and the sun. As we enter the moon sphere there comes the decision whether we shall enter earth life as a man or a woman.

Children's memories of this path

After this short description presented on the basis of Rudolf Steiner's spiritual-scientific research there will now be some sayings by children which describe quite impressively details of prenatal existence.

Looking up at the full moon little Joachim told his mother: 'That is not the moon, that is the gate I came down through.'

A four-year-old was sitting at the breakfast table with his parents and his three-year-old brother. Easy conversation was passing to and fro in the course of which the mother hinted at the phlegmatic temperament of the smaller one by saying: 'He must have taken his time, and told his brother, you go first, and I will follow you.' And she turned to the older one with the light-hearted remark: 'And so you climbed onto a ray of sunlight and slid down it into the cradle.'
  At his mother's words the boy's facial expression changed so conspicuously and he seemed to be searching so hard for words that his mother stopped short and added quickly: 'Or was it not like that?'
  The boy: 'No, no, I was *much* too light for that.'
  The mother: 'So what did you do?'
  The boy: 'First of all I, um, ran—'. He searches for a suitable word, and not finding one eventually makes up a new one of his own: 'First of all I rounded the moon. Then I was heavy enough.'
  The mother: 'And then you slid into your cradle?'
  The boy: 'No, no, then I went into mummy's little garden.'

The path to conception and pregnancy

When a human being has found his parents then, when conception takes place, what has here been called the archetypal image of the human physical body joins the fertilized human germ. The human germ will then be formed according to the spiritual prototype, which corresponds to the individual possibilities of the particular person.

The spirit-soul being (ego and sentient body), which still lives in the soul world, draws to itself the etheric forces from out of cosmic expanses, thus forming an etheric or life body. The 'package' of our moral evaluations, which we left behind at our ascent into spirit worlds, is now woven into this. This is how we bring into earth life our karma, which means the prerequisites for the reconciling of destiny which we both want to and have to carry out.

The third and fourth week of pregnancy is about the time when this spiritual-soul being now sheathed in an individual etheric body connects with the human germ in the mother's womb. At this point in time, before the spiritual-soul being of the child is more firmly attached to the mother, an event occurs which is similar to one that is experienced at the moment of crossing the threshold of death. On that occasion we looked back at a complete survey of the life just completed. Now we experience a kind of preview of what we expect to experience in the coming life. It is a general survey, not a detailed one, but a picture of the possibilities awaiting us in life. Then this moment fades from our memory.

Accepting our destiny

In special cases a kind of memory of one or another of these pictures can recur later. The following report is an instance of this. It shows clearly the firm determination the spirit-soul being has, on entering our earthly world, to maintain a positive attitude however difficult the hindrances may be.

In the second report Mrs B. has transformed this determination into a particular attitude to life.

'It was much more difficult to write it down than I had imagined. I wanted to stick as strictly as I could to the truth, but my descriptions sound to me like a delicate fabric which I am trying to reproduce with rope!'

She starts by describing the difficult life situation of her own mother who is not married, has an alcoholic partner, and has already had one miscarriage. During her second pregnancy, in about the sixth month, she feels the child in her womb kicking her vigorously, after which she is not aware of it moving any more, and it feels as though it has died. She immediately goes to the doctor, who wants to operate on her, for he thinks the child cannot be saved. She rejects this, goes to another doctor, who gives her injections and orders rest, until, some days later, the child moves again.

'I was this child.'

This child is born, but she is not beautiful to look at. One of her eyes squints, the corners of her mouth turn downwards, and later on her teeth grow crooked. She makes a sickly impression, and gets a temperature every now and again for no apparent reason. Her mother does not like showing her to people. Friends are sorry for her being so unsightly, and the only thing they admire is her blond hair.

The child wonders why adults pity her. She does not feel at all unhappy or lonely, for she lives and plays with a little brother to whom she gives things and a big brother who protects her. Only the grown-ups cannot see these brothers. Not until later does she hear that apart from the earlier miscarriage her mother had a further miscarriage after her second child.

It happened once that in the presence of the child the expression 'the end of the world' was mentioned. In bed that evening she imagined the following picture: the sun setting, the yard with its hill and its cherry trees disappearing, the linden tree in front of the balcony and herself with her little blue tin bucket all disappearing. And she was afraid that there would not be another day tomorrow. All later feelings of fear were nothing compared to this feeling of being caught up in the destruction of the world, of seeing everything she was used to holding onto disappearing – the house being razed to the ground and the trees crushed and herself swept away in the roar of the storm. A monster opens its jaws and threatens to devour the child. She screams with terror. She turns over in bed until she lies on her knees and implores: 'Dear God, do not let the world come to an end tomorrow! Let the sun come back! At least tomorrow!'

Then the whole world was transformed. A great calm was suddenly there, and a question hung in the air: 'Why?' She then entered more strongly into her own inner depths, searched for the reason why and, finding the answer, she said: 'I want to do something in the world. I have promised to do something great, and I still have to do it.' And giving this answer she felt herself to be in the centre of creation, full of love towards everything that had just appeared so destructible, but also full of a feeling of responsibility beyond all understanding.

Now, for the first time, she experienced loneliness, and wept. But then it seemed as though at the head of her bed there was seated a being clad in a wide, white robe, before whom she knelt, and laid her head on its lap, and the being spread out its wings over her.

When the child started school the moments of conviction

came less often. The child often thought of a being sitting on the right hand of her bed, but she felt as though she were merely imagining it. Admittedly the being did 'speak' to her, and she felt his presence, but less and less did she believe in what she saw. Yet she was furious when this being gave her to understand that it was not going to oblige any more but wished to withdraw. The child convinced herself that the being could not possibly withdraw, for she herself was creating it in her own thoughts. But the room became empty.

The child is perplexed, and cannot bear being deserted. Whether on that evening or later on, she resolves to believe that the being exists as long as she can only feel it. And the resolve restores her sight. The being is there again in front of her. Now, however, he stands up and moves towards the child, standing before her, joined in some mysterious way to her brow. The child felt the being as outside herself yet at the same time within her, where, with a movement of the hand, it pulled away something like a curtain which appeared to have been just inside her forehead. And for the first time the child saw the following pictures arising, like a dream, but at the same time like a long-forgotten memory.

As a grown-up, decades later, she writes: 'I am amazed that the experiences I want to narrate have not been forgotten or concealed beneath the passing years. It is more as though, closing my eyes, I were remembering something that had recently happened or, to be more exact, as though it existed right now, filling the whole of time, outside me, above me.'

And then she gropes for the right language for the memory pictures, tentatively seeking for the right feeling of responsibility for what she saw, strict with herself: 'I feel myself released from darkness. I move and this fills me with wonder, joy and the inescapable wish to continue this movement. At the edge of the darkness a being detaches himself, which accompanies me on my left. Lights emerge in front of me which move and intertwine like snakes, but which do not concern me. It seems to me that my companion wants to embrace me and carry me back into the unconscious dark. Yet I strive on towards something which looks like a spot of light. It is a plain spread out before me, picturesque and colourful.

'I am warned against my parents, especially my mother. But with all my strength I want to dive into this light. – The voice of the being now becomes clearer. I may choose between two ways: the one is to be externally beautiful but inwardly impoverished, the other to be rich and beautiful within. I choose the second way with the thought that I shall after all be able to have an influence on my exterior. Then I am surrounded by a kind of love, but also sadness. And as I depart I am allowed to make a wish. But the movement has caught me up. It appears that that itself is the wish. I experience time, feel that what lies behind me is fading away. I am alarmed and force myself to turn round. I want to be certain about my father, never lose consciousness, and bear a light within me. The joy of the being who is beside me feels like a song. Then it grows dim, after which an impressive voice tells me that I shall have a task, and I promise to remember it. As I move forward forgetfulness overcomes me, enveloping me like a cloth. Once again I call out, and this call is like a bridge which becomes as thin as a thread and hazy. Then my memory fades.'

Mrs B.: Especially as a child and in my youth I always had the feeling that I was very old, much older than my parents. For instance, I was never tempted to skip about like a lamb but was well-behaved and towed the line. But I became conscious of the situation when for example my mother asked me: 'Are you tired, shall we go home?' And without thinking I replied: 'If *you* are still enjoying yourselves let us stay!' I was horrified at my answer and my feeling of being old, but my mother did not notice. And when, as a 13-to-14-year-old I had been on my back for a whole year after many operations, accompanied by great pain, and an 'aunt' had pitied me so much she kept repeating 'poor child', I was horrified again to hear myself answering: 'That is not true at all, it is absolutely right and as it should be!' I can still see the lady's astonishment and feel my inner question: How do you know that, who has told you such a thing? I was never given an answer, but what stayed with me was the inner wakefulness and the knowledge that I should remember the question and not forget it.

Rudolf Steiner describes in his book *Theosophy* how in the higher regions of the spiritual worlds human beings gather up the intentions which they have to bring to realization in the future:

> We have to assess things differently there than we are able to do in physical life. If we have little affinity for the fine qualities that come to expression by means of for example an active thought life or wise and loving work during earthly life, we will feel this as a lack. Then we can feel an urgent need to imprint on ourselves an impulse that will cause our next life to run its course in such a way that the effect of this deficit becomes apparent in the destiny or karma we meet. The unfortunate fate—to put it in terms of that lifetime—that meets us there, and that may even provoke bitter complaining, appears in this region of the spirit as exactly what we need.

The last two reports make us feel called upon to investigate the past in our own lives too. The usual thing—despite all attempts at suppression—is to be more readily concerned about death and to cling to every conceivable possibility of survival after death. If we look back to the gate of birth and try to imagine we came from there, where our conscious memory disappears in the mists of obscurity and finally complete self-forgetfulness, the question arises more and more distinctly: Why am I in the world? What was my goal in this earthly life, and what did I undertake to do?

The moment of decision will of course not immediately disclose itself to us, however hard we rack our brains. But thinking about this question can in itself change our fundamental attitude to life. Our destiny is mirrored not only in the great events of our lives but also in the small occurrences in the daily round. Am I really awake and do I have enough presence of mind to utilize every moment, to make use, every minute, of the possibilities offered?

A great feeling of responsibility will arise in me towards my own present life. I have to go in search of ideals and aims worthy of being striven for by the human race. The more intensely I do this the nearer I shall come to the resolutions I set myself, and all the more rewarding will my own striving and its results be for humankind in general.

Reports of children's memories

Mrs R.: I can report on two experiences I had which have to do with my son Christian. He was born in Berlin in August 1945 when I myself was 24 years of age. A while before his birth—unfortunately I cannot say how many weeks before then, for the first experience was a long time ago. However, I remember it very well because it made a strong impression on me. The dream situation brought it home to me that it was very important to me. So, as I said, I dreamt a while before the birth of my son that I was walking through a bright, light-flooded landscape, with a lot of bushes and trees. I heard a child's voice calling me and I knew it was my son. I looked for him behind the bushes, but I could not find him.

So before his birth I only heard his voice.

The second experience was like this. When my son was four years old he said to me one day: 'Before I was born I was sitting on your roof all the time and looking down at you.'

Mrs A.: 'Mummy, it really was very difficult to come to you.'

Her mother gives him a querying look.

'From above, I mean. An angel brought me, carrying me on his back. Then I slipped into your tummy and closed the entrance again,' – pause. Then: 'During the time I was with you I kept all the devils away from you.'

Right from the beginning of pregnancy great changes take place in the woman's organism. Pregnant women acquire a specially beautiful, harmonious facial expression. They appear to us as though touched by a breath of heaven – and this is indeed so.

Mrs E.: Three-and-a-half-year-old J. told me one day: 'Above the sky there is another sky, and that is where I was. I wanted to come earlier, but that was not possible, because an aeroplane was in the way' (at this earlier time his mother had been engaged as a travel-guide in Greece taking care of air passengers), 'but then I did this' (he boxes with his fists) 'and then I came!'

Later on: 'Shall I tell you something else about heaven? I actually came to earth with the Virgin Mary. When Christmastime came I was actually Mary's child, and only after that was I yours.' (Around this time, as a single mother, she was simply not prepared to believe that she was pregnant.)

Mrs B. tells us about her child saying the following:

'Actually I did not at all want to come to earth then. Thomas was meant to be first. But Thomas promised me he would come too.'

Mrs I.: Johanna, three-and-a-half years old, during a conversation on how she came to me: 'Oh, first of all it was so wet, then it was dry, and then I tumbled out!'

Children do not remember separate scenes before birth, or how they descended from supersensible worlds. It is often just short flashes in which, if the grown-ups around the child have enough presence of mind, they can catch these statements. Such flashes can bring us amazing details.

It is typical that most of these statements about pre-earthly conditions are made by children under four. Normally our memory reaches back to the fourth year of life, not very often to the third, before which it is dark. We can judge from this that the baby and toddler still live in a kind of dream and are not fully conscious, yet the most determinative things of life happen during these first years. Children begin to take hold of the world. They learn to stand upright and to maintain their balance whilst standing and walking. They learn to imitate speech, and finally to think. So this taking hold of their own bodies and their environment happens quite unconsciously. The way they crawl, stand up, speak, the whole way they move, is different with every child; it is individual. It can perhaps be described like this: the being, the individuality of the child forms the growing body as though from outside and is still entirely under the influence of the beings who led it into the world.

Because children's consciousness of this world is not yet fully developed their memory can still reach back into the world they came from.

Presentiments in the Circle of Relatives

This presentation of the prenatal existence of human beings shows how important is the connection with the generations of ancestors, how intimate is the relationship to the people among whom they want to incarnate. Infinite love and trust is felt for those people. This can be sensed in many of the reports. Seen from this aspect, the love that comes towards the newborn baby from the people close to it — especially the proverbial mother love — is a return for the love coming directly from the child. Such a viewpoint does not in any way belittle mother love but can on the contrary possibly be a help in freeing it from its foolish, sometimes almost animal-like components. Mother love and the love we bring to the child is not a biological and automatic matter but one with a real spiritual foundation. So it is not surprising that the coming human being also announces its arrival in advance to the circle of relatives lovingly awaiting it.

Mrs D. (sister of Mrs E. and the mother of F.): F. was so much in touch with me in particular that for a long time I had the feeling he actually wanted to come to me.

It was like this. Shortly after the birth of my sister's third son, I believe it was only about three weeks later, I dreamt I was in a garage-like building where along the walls stood the four beds of my sister's four boys. I entered this bunker and looked at the boys. I recognized my sister's two eldest sons, and they smiled at me. The third son lay among the pillows and his face was white with no facial features (for in reality I had not yet seen him), and in the fourth bed I could see nothing. I did not even recognize the bed, and there were no outlines — nothing. Nevertheless I knew *quite definitely* there is another one there, my sister's fourth boy. He was virtually compelling me to be aware of him, without being visible.

I told my sister about it at the time, although I was almost ashamed to do so in view of the difficult birth of her third son, and she shrugged it aside with a sigh. Mrs E. became pregnant soon after that, and had her fourth son.

Mrs D.: S, my sister's first son, had just been born when I dreamt that I and my sister were together in a large kitchen where there was work going on. Ironing was being done on a big table. Beside the table was a cot in which my sister's two boys were sitting, different in size, being about one and two years old respectively. They were sitting side by side leaning against the long side of the cot watching what was going on. They were wearing national costume jackets with red and green edges like our mother actually made for them later on, just like those. What I can still remember well is the broadness of their faces, exactly as my sister's children looked later.

Mr H.: When one of our daughters-in-law was expecting a baby my wife said to me one morning on waking: 'Our grandchild is there, and it is a boy. I dreamt he came skipping up to me in my dream and told me with great joy: My name is Andreas!' Soon after we had got up the telephone rang and our son informed us that his wife had just given birth to a boy.

Mrs Sch. reports her dream about her grandchild who is on the way. She had the dream three weeks before the child was born:

I saw a fully grown, well-formed child moving with little rocking movements in the clear foetal fluid, and I could see it through a thin, delicate covering. It held its head above water and looked at me as though it knew me very well. I spoke to it and said: 'I often think of you even when I am painting.' 'I know, I know, that is lovely!' it replied. 'But do you know, I hardly have any more room to swim. Sometimes I would like to have already been born, but I have a feeling that is difficult too.'

As it said this it looked at me solemnly. Then I told it I would like to recite something for it, and so it listened: 'To wonder at beauty, to nurture the truth ... (prayer at the ringing of the evening bells). I felt that the child was continuing to listen, as though it wanted to hear more. So I went on reciting: 'Thou art in everything—let thy most glorious light, O Lord, touch my face...' The child kept still, and there was a mood of trust and courage between us. The picture slowly dissolved into silvery-blue water.

Reports from the parents' circle of friends

A wider circle of people around the parents can also be included in the event of the coming to earth of a human being. People who are attached to the parents in deep friendship get to hear of the coming child. Now and again there do not seem to be such close ties, or it is only through these events that one is made aware of them. In the spiritual world there appear to be other criteria for judging our earthly relationships.

Ch. had been happily married for ten years, but despite an ardent wish to have a child she has not had one. She invites her female friends to her birthday. She knew from her doctor, just the day before, that she is at last expecting a child, but she intends to keep it a secret. Then her closest friend says to her in front of everyone else: 'Do you know what I dreamt? You had had a son, and he was called Peter. And I was holding him at his christening.'

So Ch. had to tell her friends her secret.

Mrs D.: Ursula has been my friend since my childhood. She has two boys of twelve and ten and a daughter, Michaela, seven years old. Michaela is my godchild.

One night I dreamt I heard a child crying up in the attic. It was the attic in my mother's house. I went up and saw a boy of about three standing there crying his heart out. His name was Franz. I picked him up and said: 'Do not cry. I will take you to your sister Michaela'. And so the boy was comforted. At the time I did not know what to make of the dream. A while later Ursula told me joyfully that she had confirmation that she was pregnant. Then the scales fell from my eyes. I told her about my dream, yet she did not call the boy Franz.

Mrs K.: I gave support to a young man who was going blind. When he had become completely blind he got married. In due course his wife expected a child, but she was very worried for she had developed myeloma, and this she confided to me.

As a consequence of this I dreamt that a beautiful girl was standing in front of me with an oval face and fair hair, and she was weaving on a little loom from the bottom upwards. It was set up in front of the child and had the shape of a lyre. Eventually a child really was born, and it looked just like this.

A few years later the mother told me hesitantly that she was possibly expecting another child, although she was not in good health. Thereupon I heard in a dream, 'This will be a little Joseph,' and I told the mother of the dream. Later on the woman had a delicate baby boy.

Mrs N.: One of the things I would like to tell you happened shortly before the birth of Raphaele, my friend's child. My friend stayed with us for four weeks. At that time our daughter had just turned two and had developed a special relationship to my friend.

During the last few days before the baby's birth my daughter said four times, when we went upstairs to my friend's room: 'Mummy, a child from heaven' and usually pointed up into a corner of the ceiling. But when she was lifted up she stopped pointing.

After my friend had had the baby in hospital she did not say it any more.

Mrs L.: An acquaintance of mine had been hoping for a child for many years. Both she and her husband had organic difficulties which made it difficult for a pregnancy to come about. I knew her for almost three years and we had often spoken about this worry. One night she told me in a dream that she was expecting a child, a son. She was ill at the time, which discouraged me from speaking about my dream. But a few weeks later she confirmed the pregnancy.

B. had been a probationer with Mrs E. for six weeks. She was very happy there, and occasionally went on a visit after the course was over. More than a year later she writes and tells her that she dreamt Mrs E. was having her fifth child. Mrs E. was then already in the fourth month of pregnancy.

Mrs T.: I love painting, especially children. I usually do not know what will arise – I just let it come. I painted a fairly large picture of a child for each of several families I was friendly with. It transpired that if I had painted a girl the family had a girl in the course of that year, or a boy if I had painted a boy.

For another young couple I painted two children—a boy who was larger, and a girl. They had twins, of which the boy was born first.

Mrs T. reports: On October 1, I had this dream about a family I was friends with. The housewife stood at the large round table in their dining room, and she laid out on it a white baby jacket and a little pink frock to show me. I was being told in this way that she was expecting a baby. Then at the end of January her fifth child was born, much loved by its older sisters, and I am delighted that I shall be the godmother.

People who have experiences of this kind can feel themselves included in the intentions of the spiritual world in an obviously planned course of action. And it will be borne home to them that they bear a responsibility for the children wanting to come.

All of us carry a responsibility for the well-being of the generations succeeding us. Whether a country welcomes children or not depends on all of us. What is decisive is whether a new understanding can grow for the actual incarnating process of a human being.

But it does not depend solely on an attitude of joyful welcome in general, but on an understanding of child nature. We must take care to see that as many as possible of the abilities and inclinations the children want to bring into earthly life can become effective. The children's environment, education and school must be arranged accordingly. For instance, abstract thinking at too early an age can hinder healthy development, whereas the pictures in fairy tales are nourishment for the soul.

Western culture needs comprehensive renewal. This can come only from spiritual regions from whence the children themselves also come. We must take care to see that these new impulses can actually enter into our world.

If we look at destiny and karmic laws in the right way we do not arrive at fatalism, but feel ourselves called upon to help see that everybody's destiny can be carried out, that hardships are lessened and borne, that blockages can be detected, so that the progress of humankind is helped altogether.

Abortions and contraception from the viewpoint of the unborn child

Contraception and abortion already existed in earlier times. Nowadays they are almost taken for granted, in fact they are frequently considered as a necessary prerequisite for a life worthy of a human being. We shall go into this more fully later (see pp. 213ff). The following description shows us what the immediate reaction is of a sensitive mother to a suggested abortion.

Mrs W.: When the gynaecologist offered me an abortion for a fourth child as though it were the obvious thing, something rebelled inside me (although financially we were in a very bad way). Straight away and for a considerable time I had the feeling that I would need to give this child particularly strong protection. We subsequently followed the development of this child from its birth onwards with particular awareness, just as though we had discovered the seedling of a plant in a flower pot or in a bed in the garden and were to observe it daily, not in the way a scientist has to do it but with both awe and intimacy.

In the next two examples it is little children again, remembering prenatal situations.

Mrs L.: My mother told me the following. We have a small brother — an afterthought — who, in his early childhood, did not have a proper relationship with his mother. During an illness when he was three years old and running a high temperature, the problem was solved. In his delirium he said that his mother had kept on pushing him back into the water.

Before his birth his mother had had several abortions.

Mrs A.: While I was busy cooking, Johanna, two-and-three-quarter years old, told me the following:

'There was once a mummy and her name was Anya. And there was a sister called Britt. And the mummy threw me out of the window into the dustbin. And the father was called Marcus.'

Mother: 'Really?'

Johanna: 'Yes, they simply threw me out of the window! Then I looked through your window (she hugged me), and so I had a nice mummy, and you let me in (hugged me really tightly). You really are my mummy, aren't you?'

Mother: 'Where was this, Johanna?'

Johanna: 'In a little black house so big' (showing with her finger how small it was).

Mrs L. already had two children. Both for economic and personal reasons the family did not want any more children. Therefore she had a coil fitted.

Mrs L.: In the case of my third child there were not only no psychological symptoms but there were no physical symptoms at all either. In the third month it needed the doctor to confirm that I was pregnant. (Even he was surprised, as he had said that a pregnancy was almost impossible.) I was so upset that I had difficulty in welcoming it. More than was the case with my other children I felt that the decision had been made in the spiritual realm; a child had resolved to incarnate, and so I overcame all the hindrances.

During the pregnancy I was tormented by fears and apprehensions. The only consolation was actually the certainty that although my third child was a pregnancy with risks, it would be born healthy.

At birth my daughter was the largest and heaviest of my children. Looking at her then, who would have guessed that after a few short months she would be hypersensitive and delicate?

Long after the birth of our daughter my husband reminded me of my long-forgotten dream. A little girl wanted to come in through the front door. Because it was locked she tried to come through the kitchen window. But the only way she could come in was through the keyhole.

This last dream image is too obvious to need any further explanation, but we do see the utter determination of the child, in fact the necessity driving her to be born to these parents in particular. We can sense the agitation in the soul world bordering on ours when a human being is trying to come down into incarnation.

'And you shall be my mother!'

In the following example, despite the fact that there was obviously a strong tie between the unborn child and the chosen mother, she decides against giving birth to it.

Mrs B.: Last summer we spent the holidays on the Atlantic coast. One day I went for a long walk on the beach by myself. It was in the afternoon. I took off my shoes and walked for miles barefoot on the wonderful sandy beach.

The tide was just coming in, and the sea flowed over the sand steadily and rhythmically, moving forwards and backwards, and as I walked I was aware of it, and listened to the water. I looked at the far distance where the sky and the water melted into one another, and both the elements shimmered and sparkled in the most dazzling sunlight. I was transported into a kind of trance, a state between waking and sleeping. My perception was focused on the rhythm of the waves, my steps and on the light on the horizon when, all of a sudden, I saw a face in front of me, very indistinct and blurred. I walked on looking firmly at this apparition. It was the face of a little girl of about four or five. The clearest thing I could see were the eyes, which were very large and expressive. What happened then is difficult to put into words. This child actually spoke to me, yet—just as in the dream I had had when I was pregnant with my daughter—the child's lips did not move. I cannot say either that I heard her speak. It was rather that I felt quite clearly what she wanted to say. And what she said was: 'I am Maria, and you shall be my mother!'

I must add at this point that I did not have the desire at the time to have another child, and up till that moment I had not thought about it at all.

So a whole flood of thoughts and feelings took hold of me. I did not answer the child consciously, but I knew that all the time she could hear and understand everything I was thinking and feeling. First of all came a tremendous feeling of happiness, immense joy, but it then occurred to me that I did not want another child at all, at least not now so quickly after the first two. I thought it was much too soon, and that I should not become pregnant again already, because I needed all my strength for my other two children. And I am not a good mother if I constantly overwork. I told myself that I needed more time, and should wait another couple of years. Then the child 'said': 'I want to be born!' I felt that she was unhappy. And I thought: 'Why do you want to be born, now, when any day a terrible war can break out on the earth, and we would all have to suffer and die? I can hardly bear these thoughts, when I look at my children and imagine this horror. Wait a while, do wait, and perhaps everything will be better soon, and human beings will learn to live together in peace. I cannot right now give birth to you. I neither can nor want to!'

Suddenly it was all over. I stood still and looked at the sand. I endeavoured to see my way and think clearly again. Then I noticed I was crying. I was terribly confused and sad.

Mrs B., up till now the mother of two children, has not had another child since.

Children are led to other parents

The following reports show clearly how consistently human beings can be led. If the path to their rightful parents is blocked by unsurmountable obstacles then other ways are found, or the original plan can even still come about in a roundabout way. These reports speak quite clearly for themselves, and need no further clarification.

O.J. Hartmann reports in his book on medical-pastoral psychology: A four-year-old said to his aunt: 'Do you know, Auntie, I should actually have come to you.'

We can imagine the grown-up's disconcerted 'What do you mean by that?' And Renate, as the child was called, went on:

'You see, it was like this. I was with a lot of other people a long way away from the earth, in heaven. And suddenly an old man came and called out: "Go, Renate, you have to go down now!'' And so it started up. I was whirled around the earth. That went in all directions so incredibly fast. And then I passed by your window, but I could not get in. So I flew further, and Mummy's window was open, and I could get in there. And so I came to Mummy, but actually I should have come to you!'

There was another child who after being born by way of illegitimate paternity as a kind of outsider in a family and subsequently given away was then sent by the Child Welfare Office to various foster homes. It was finally adopted by a childless couple. The morning after its first night in its new home, it says to its new mother while being dressed:

'Mummy, I always wanted to come to you, but the little door was shut!'

Mrs D.: I had a further dream which gave me a lot to think about. I was on an excursion with a group of people I do not know. My children had come along, but I did not actually see them or my husband. The group and I stopped to rest in a sloping meadow. As we set out again there was a boy with Down syndrome playing with a small cart. He was about ten years old. One of the group asked whom he belonged to, and I said word for word: 'That is our Peter. He has to come with us.' I put him into the cart and on we went.

The pregnancy which began soon after that ended in a miscarriage. And when the doctor told me that nature often corrects itself by getting rid of what is not going to develop properly, I remembered my dream and it all became clear to me.

Yet it was not all that clear after all. Years later I was offered, by telephone, two foster children to choose from. There were no criteria, so I asked what their names were and was told Gunnar and Peter. Without recalling my dream in the least I chose Peter, because I preferred the name. How otherwise was I to 'choose' a child, when they were both the same age, both came from impossible backgrounds, and I had never seen either of them?

So now we have 'our Peter' after all, a boy with great learning difficulties and whose appearance has a slight tendency towards Down syndrome. He has no sense for numbers, in fact he cannot even count (up to 29 with difficulty), and although he is nine-and-a-half he is like a six-year-old, not only physically. My feelings towards him in the dream were just the same as they are in reality: a strong feeling of belonging, but more rational than emotional, as though it was destined to happen. I regard this boy as our destiny, and could not imagine giving him away. There is a bond; he never strikes me as being a stranger, although I am not at all particularly attached to him.

Mrs D.: The dream. The bell rang downstairs and it was for our flat. So I opened it. A little girl about four years old stood in front of me, a small, slender child. 'You cannot come in just now,' I said, 'Juergen is busy painting his pictures.'

'Yes I can,' said the little one, 'Hannchen has to be there as well.' And she pushed past me, forcefully using her elbows. The first-mentioned name belongs to our adopted child who had been with us just over a year by then. He came to us when he was six months old. We wanted to have a little girl as well, but we were in no hurry. Yet I told my husband the next morning that the little girl had got in touch, and we ought to look for her. And I told him the dream. A second adoption went faster. The procedure for the adoption of Juergen a year before was still warm, and the formalities simpler than today (1937).

So I found our child very quickly. I got hold of the

address of the guardianship office. There were two small girls available for adoption in a children's home. The matron showed me a one-year-old child with blond curls and blue eyes and intelligent, in fact a superb specimen. And the matron was annoyed when I turned her down. What on earth did I want, if I did not want this child! All I could say was that it was not my child.

And the other child. She was eight weeks old, very delicate and small, with two deep worry furrows, and such huge eloquent eyes with which she held my gaze. I have never seen such wide-awake eyes at such a tender age before. After I had said goodbye the eyes drew me to them once again. I went up to the little child and said, 'Just wait, I will definitely come and fetch you, it will not take long.' I believe she understood me, for it was in fact little Hannchen. And she brought along her little pointed elbows for pushing with, as a proof.

That is the most beautiful experience I have ever had, and to this day I still marvel at the miracle of it. She became our much beloved child.

MAX HOFFMEISTER

Human Nature – Existence Before Birth – Reincarnation

The Problem

During a sitting of the German Bundestag [parliament] on 25 April 1974, a delegate made the following statement:

> Both of these aspects — and this is a painful realization — are purely relative: the right to have a different assessment with regard to the various stages of pregnancy, either in favour of the mother as an individual or in favour of the child's right to live. Spelt out, this means on the one hand the relative position of the mother's increasingly receding right to self-determination with regard to the various stages of pregnancy, and the just as relative increasingly predominating right of the child to life at these different stages. Only if we consider each of these conflicting judgements according to their respective importance at each stage shall we do justice to this conflict of values in a way that befits the basic values of our constitution. This means having the same respect for human dignity and the responsible self-determination of the woman on the one hand as for the child's right to life on the other, and the securing and maintaining of the rights of each at every stage of the pregnancy...

In this question of the interruption of pregnancy, which was the topic of this sitting of the Bundestag, the two opposing factors were the aspect of the mother and the aspect of the child, i.e. the embryonic development of the human seed. On the one side there is paragraph 218, forbidding interruption of pregnancy — abortion — which consists of separate paragraphs and is in the Book of Civil Law, and on the other side abortion is defended in arguments taken from the fundamental law of the constitution and consists of a series of articles.

The first part of the fundamental law concerns basic rights (Articles 1–19). This says:

Article 1, paragraph 1:
'The dignity of man is inviolable...'

Article 2, paragraph 1:
'Everyone has the right to a free unfolding of their personality in so far as they do not violate the rights of others or infringe on the constitutional order or the moral code.'

Paragraph 2:
'Everyone has the right to life and bodily inviolation. The freedom of the person is inviolable. These rights are unalterable except by law.'

It is worthy of note for what follows that what we hear about is always rights, even if these are sometimes within limits. We seldom hear of obligations, in fact we only hear on one occasion directly of duty, and this is in the Fundamental Laws in Article 6, paragraph 2 with regard to that of the parents. In the above-mentioned statements during the Bundestag debate the inviolable dignity of man (Article 1, 1) and the free unfolding of the personality (Article 2, 1) are brought in connection with the right to self-determination of the mother. According to Michael Debus[1] recently, this train of thought goes back to the Koenigsberg philosopher Immanuel Kant (1724–1804), who still influences modern thinking, and who said in his *Kritik der reinen Vernunft* in 1781: 'Autonomy (= self-determination) is the basis for the dignity of man and for every creature of reason.'

Or, in other words: 'My tummy belongs to me.'

A child developing in its mother's womb still has the right to life (Article 2, 2) but it is not as yet assigned any human dignity. Therefore human dignity as the right to self-determination, the right to freedom (Article 2, 1) gives the mother the legal right to interrupt the pregnancy.

But neither the body itself, neither that of the pregnant mother nor that of the child, is the expression and the foundation of human dignity in itself, though it paves the way for it. In their time the Romans said, '*Sit mens sana in corpore sano*,' which means, freely translated: 'It is only in a healthy body that the spirit can unfold healthily.'

Is it really by means of our body that we live in a 'humanly dignified manner'? In other words, do we use our body in order to live in a way that is worthy of a human being? So it is the body then, both that of the mother and that of the child within its mother's womb, which has to be protected and preserved (Article 2, 2: bodily inviolation), because it belongs to the requisites for possible human dignity. However, dignity and freedom do not mutually exclude one another, unless we take freedom to mean self-seeking wilfulness, an opportunity to indulge ourselves. Surely we are only truly free if, out of insight for the necessities of life and the environment we constantly think in a responsible way. This kind of attitude and action based on freedom includes the fact that out of insight (in clear distinction from Kant's moral duty) we are also prepared to make renunciations.

We are only too willing to understand self-realization as an unrestrained, egoistic freedom to indulge ourselves, though unfortunately this is often at the expense of others. And how is this resolved with regard to a child's right to life, of a human being in the becoming? From what moment onwards is the seed in the mother's womb to be considered a person? Even as grown-ups are we not all still in a process of becoming, only on the way to becoming human? For surely until we reach the stage of human dignity the very concept cannot yet apply to us? The body belongs to the prerequisites of *potential* dignity. And from when onwards? This is in the first place a natural-scientific question, so first we will turn to this.

The Natural-scientific Aspect

From the point of view of genetics the human being is considered a person from conception onwards, i.e. from the moment of the union of the ovum with the sperm. The fructified ovum then has a double (diploid) set of chromosomes, as have all the following body cells out of which the embryo gradually grows. The human being's hereditary 'instructions' consisting of 2 × 23 chromosomes are entirely human. A mother has never yet produced a rabbit, because each animal has a different set of chromosomes — its own hereditary instructions belonging to its species. Due to the typically formed X- and Y-chromosomes it is at least already determined in the line of heredity whether a boy (with XY-chromosomes) will be born or a girl (with XX-chromosomes). So from the aspect of genetics the embryo which has been set in train has begun right from the outset to develop in the human direction.

Erich Blechschmidt,[2] the Goettingen human embryologist, followed up the development of embryos in the first stages and came to the conclusion that right from the beginning this development is different from that of animals. It is also generally known that with animals, even monkeys, the embryonic bubble-like structure (the blastula, which develops in humans six days after conception) does not consist of round cells as in humans, but flattened ones, i.e. specialized ones.[3] Furthermore, in the second week of pregnancy when the embryo is already implanted in the uterus, in the case of human beings the space between the embryonic knot in which the organization of the body will be developing — from the seventeenth day onwards — and the position of the chorion[4] is filled with mesenchyme, a substance which contains a number of unattached cells, whilst in the case of animals (even anthropoid apes) mesodermal structures are visible.[5] Embryonic animal development consequently shows at a much earlier stage than in humans the presence of thoroughly structured tissues with specialized cells, as though the human being was not in such a hurry to pin down and fix the form of its developing body.[6]

And there is a further thing. Characteristic of human embryonic development is the fact that right up to the end of the second month one cannot distinguish externally whether the embryo will turn out to be a girl or a boy. For the urogenital system, i.e. the formation of the kidneys and the sexual organs, arises from a common organ layout in the case of both a boy or a girl. Right up to the end of the embryonic period (seven to eight weeks) the human being is hermaphrodite, which means it has the tendency to be both masculine and feminine at the same time.[7] It is like it was in the case of Adam, who did not become male until Eve, the female element, was separated from him. At the beginning Adam was purely human, without defined sexual characteristics. At the end of the second month the embryo, which already has a human form, still conforms to the archetypal human image.

So during embryonic development human beings hold back from sexual differentiation until towards the end of the second month, despite the fact that, in having either XY-chromosomes or XX- chromosomes they are genetically sexually predetermined right from the beginning. When the sexual differentiating occurs at the end of the second month the embryo,[8] although barely 3 cm long, is fully formed as a human being, even to its inner organization. All it needs to do is grow larger. The step from the second to the third month is the moment when the embryo becomes a foetus.

When it is stated that this structure barely 3 cm in length is only a clump of mucus, that is correct with regard to its consistency, its material content being about 95% water. Yet this delicate structure, which is still as soft as a jellyfish, not only has a human form with a relatively large head and high forehead and even an already clearly formed nose, etc., but also contains a fully developed cartilage skeleton which in many places has already begun to ossify.[9] But just as in small children the bones are still really soft, so that if they fall down they rarely break them, we can imagine that the gristly frame of this 3–4 cm long foetus is at the beginning of the third month still much softer than in a newborn baby. However, the essential thing is that this small foetus already has a fully human form. Therefore it should certainly not be described as an indeterminate clump of mucus.

As we saw, a typical characteristic of being human is the holding back of development so as not to arrive too quickly at fixed forms. As a mother's milk for its human offspring contains fewer nutrients than the mother's milk of animals, a human child also grows more slowly. The doubling of its birth weight happens with humans only after four months, whereas with horses it happens already after two months, with sheep after a fortnight, and with dogs after only nine days.

With human beings puberty does not occur until 11–16 years of age, although the sexual organs have already finished developing by the end of the fifth year. Whilst mammals are already capable of procreating as soon as the organs have developed,[10] in the case of human beings early maturity is hindered by the presence of melatonin, a hormone excreted by the pineal gland (epiphysis cerebri) so that the growing youngster will have become sufficiently stabilized to be capable of acting with responsibility and judgement and no longer be at the mercy of uncontrolled urges. In contrast to animals human beings have further years of life ahead of them after their capacity to procreate has ceased, in which they can also develop further mentally and spiritually. So we see that, all round, the human growing process points both to holding back from premature fixation and also to a holding back from final completeness. The human being as a human being is never finished, but is always in the process of becoming. Yet right from the beginning we are on our way to becoming human. At every stage we have the possibility within us to stand up for our human dignity. We are already human right from the stage of germ cell.

The Spiritual Aspect

The ego and ego consciousness

What do we understand altogether by the words 'human being'? When I say, 'I feel myself to be a human being,' surely I can only say so when I am fully awake. We feel we identify with our body, as a unity. When on the other hand we are tired in the evening a distinctly different feeling arises, as though we were shattered, broken. We drag ourselves around, and feel as though we were broken in two. If some sudden impression *awakens* our interest (presence) our tiredness vanishes. We are 'all there' again. But until this happens we are not conscious of it. Similarly we do not know until we wake up that we have been asleep, for while we are asleep we have no self-perception and therefore no awareness of ourselves. We now and then notice in our dream on awakening that we are coming as though from a long way away, for example over some water to the shore, or we are feeling our way along passages or down a chimney or careering down a tower when we wake up suddenly. These passages, chimney or tower are in this case pictures of our inner life processes.

Who or what is this ego which only becomes conscious of itself when in the physical body? For when we speak of our ego we do so with that wide-awake consciousness of ours which is dependent on the physical body. This body was there yesterday just as it is today, and it must have been there when we slept during the night too, even if we knew nothing about it. For it was only our ego-*consciousness* that was not there, just as our thinking, feeling and willing did not exist any more, consciously, either.

In essence, then, our ego must be something which as

such is always there yet which in the course of the day repeatedly disappears to a greater or lesser extent from our consciousness. So what we perceive is actually only our ego-consciousness. During sleep it is as though our whole soul life were extinguished. So it is only what we perceive that we grasp consciously. This consciousness can either be very clear and definite or it can just flit by like a shadow. It can even happen that what we perceive may not be consciously grasped, 'it went too fast', or 'we were not paying attention'. Now and then it descends straight away into the subconscious, and swings to and fro out of the depths of the soul to the surface of consciousness. This oscillating, surging field of consciousness is in the narrower, more actual sense what the soul is. In ancient times popular belief had it that the soul – as distinct from the earth-bound body – was a being in movement, the image of which they saw as a butterfly or a bird.[11] In ancient Egypt the soul Ba was represented as a bird. In the Greek language the word soul is indicated phonetically by the word *aiolos*, which means 'in movement', 'in rapid oscillation'.[12] Soul nature has always been felt as something labile and in restless movement. To be able to see things in the light of the spirit one needs to struggle through to soul calm, which can be pictured as a calming of a storm (e.g. in Mark 4: 35–41). Then we see the world and our own selves in a smooth mirror undisturbed. In our ordinary soul life, which is normally in movement, our ego-consciousness surges back and forth and up and down.

What persists is the ego, by means of which we remember our activities of the previous day, thus maintaining the continuity of our experience of existence. This continuous element often felt as the observing part of us – the part that is active in our memory – has since former times been described as a spiritual principle. While in our soul element we are caught up in movement in a more passive way, often being exposed powerlessly to the surging waves of sympathy and antipathy, when we take firm hold of the reins we feel the ego-force as an active higher principle in us. Think of the famous bronze statue of the charioteer in Delphi. In the *Bhagavadgita* it is the god Krishna himself who accompanies the human being, Prince Arjuna, as his charioteer and gives him instruction.

But the ego-force is often insufficient, and now and then it is as though our actual ego looked sadly down, as a higher being, onto the wild soul turbulence in our breast. In primeval times, when this individual 'I' was as yet not so deeply united with the body, it was felt to be the actual spiritual being which overshadowed the body.

The body-soul problem in psychosomatics

We are interpolating something here which is known by the name of psychosomatics,[13] the body-soul problem, and which over the past 40 years has gradually become recognized in the realm of official medicine — particularly in connection with psychosomatic medicine.

The best-known example of this problem is the psycho-somatically caused stomach ulcer whereby a stomach operation is ineffective, because a stomach ulcer returns again, or other symptoms develop such as asthma, general debility or depression. Unless the doctor sends the patient to a psychotherapist he will recommend a change of attitude.[14]

Why does a person get a stomach complaint? One possible reason is if fresh demands are made on him and he constantly has the feeling he cannot satisfy his colleagues. Or because of an ambitious will to achieve, the feeling is constantly boring into him: 'My life has not been the success I hoped it would be.'[15]

It is soul sensations such as worry, suppression and constant annoyance that make him ill. His ego-consciousness is apparently not strong enough to see these in themselves unnecessary feelings clearly and to put them aside and replace them by acquiring self-confidence. And a person can only do this out of strengthened ego-force. A psychosomatic doctor can recommend him to take up this approach. What he has to do then is to achieve the feat of applying sufficient ego-wakefulness and insight to draw into his constitution his own higher ego, the spiritual core of his being, so as to counteract therapeutically the ill effects of his misguided soul being.

In other words: if the person can take hold of himself better his ego-force grows in his soul. If he cannot do this alone his fellow human beings must help him. With the help of understanding, praise, acknowledgment of him as a person, his self-confidence can be aroused. This is important too, in the education of children, to give praise where it is justified, for too much criticism — especially nowadays — can be destructive.

Even though this body-soul problem is certainly recognized today, too little attention is still given to the fact that it is after all the ego, the active spiritual element in the human being, that has to be called in.[16] The life of the soul is often felt to be the helpless, suffering part of our being. Either the doctor or some other knowledgable person can appeal to the patient's or fellow human being's ego to take action against the destructive course of the illness.

Thus where psychosomatics is concerned there arises not only the question of looking for the causes in the soul realm but also the ongoing question: How does one get the patient to put spiritual participation, his actual ego, to work to take better hold of his body so that healing by way of his own strength — self-healing — can come about altogether?[17]

What we are concerned with here is actually a problem

of spirit, soul and body, where the spiritual ingredient, as the active principle, is in charge of the body and can have a healing effect upon it. A similar action takes place during sleep when our soul life has ceased its activity in the body, and this is why sleep has such a health-bringing and restorative effect.

Concerning threefoldness

Our previous observations show that we may look at human beings as consisting of body, soul and spirit. The soul is the part of them that intermittently becomes conscious, like a field of consciousness between the spiritual part of their being, their ego and their physical, bodily part. The ego, as the spiritual core of our being, takes hold of the physical body, on waking for instance, and becomes more or less self-aware in our thinking, feeling and will. This threefold membering of the being in body, soul and spirit, already known in olden times, is called the trichotomy. The word trichotomy means: an existence cut into three, a threefold membering.

We experience other people when they are awake as more or less distinct *personalities*. What 'sounds' forth from the body (*personare*) is the individuality,[18] the spiritual core of the person, the actual ego.

Goethe spoke of the entelechy of the human being as coming from the Greek word *entelekheia*, coined by Aristotle (384–322 BC) and meaning a being who has his goal (*telos*) in (*en*) himself (*ekhei*). The poet Christian Morgenstern said in similar vein:

Wer vom Ziel nichts weiss,
kann den Weg nicht haben...
(If you know nothing of the goal you cannot find the
   way...)

and Goethe's friend F.W. Riemer (1774–1845) wrote in his diary:

> To my question as to what Goethe was conveying in his homunculus Eckermann told me that Goethe was presenting entelechy as such, the spirit of man, as he appears in life before he has begun to gain experience. For the spirit of a human being arrives highly gifted. By no means do we learn everything, but bring it with us.

Occasionally we know very well what would be the right thing to do, but the desire nature in our soul drives us in another direction which we feel is not right, and yet we do not follow our feeling for the truth but defend our wrongdoing with our rational mind. We say casually: Our better self actually says 'No'. This actual self which knows better was called by Socrates (470–399 BC), Plato's teacher, his daemon (Greek *Daimōn*).[19] It constantly warns us, but never tells us, what we ought to do—that is left to the freedom of our ego-conscious self which makes its own judgements.

Whereas the Latin word for human being is *homo*, which has a similar stem etymologically to humus, meaning the soil of the earth, and thus expresses the earthly aspect, the Greek word *anthropos* refers to someone who looks upwards, indicating the soul aspect. The basic stem of the word *Mensch*, which exists among the Germanic languages, points to the spiritual aspect. The Gothic word *Mannaseths* in the Wulfila Bible (*c.* AD 350) means humankind, though literally translated it means spirit seed.[20] The meaning of the word human being is therefore spirit bearer.

And this was how Goethe understood it and, remarkably, this came to expression in his last conversation with Eckermann on 11 March 1832, i.e. eleven days before he died:

In all its appearances what is it and what is it going to become? At the conclusion of the well-known imagination of the six days of creation God certainly did not rest but continued to be active as on the first day. To put this crude world together out of simple elements and set it rolling in the rays of the sun, year in year out, would have given him no pleasure at all if he had not had the plan to found, on the basis of this material foundation, a nursery for a world of spirits. Thus he is continuously active in higher natures, for the purpose of educating the lesser ones.

Grasping the spiritual element is the most difficult of all. For a consciousness of the reality of the spirit, even if formerly this was more dreamlike, is something we have lost more and more in the course of time as our waking consciousness has been developing. Since the eighth ecumenical Council of Constantinople in the year AD 869, it was solely permitted to say that a human being possesses a body in which there is a soul which only has certain spiritual qualities.

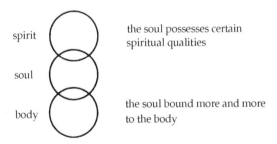

spirit

soul

body

the soul possesses certain spiritual qualities

the soul bound more and more to the body

By that time the spiritual element itself was in fact no longer felt by human beings to be a part of their lives. And it is still so today. It seems to us that it merely overshadows us and is no longer active within us in a real way. What people came more and more to experience as the active ingredient in them was their conscious soul life, when they were united with the body during the daytime. And people eventually spoke of a body-soul dualism.

As it was only with the body-bound consciousness that in the end any reality was accredited to soul experience – spirit had already completely disappeared from consciousness, and it was only in the thinking realm that a shadowy presentiment of it still existed – research therefore was now focused on the body. And Ernst Haeckel made the pronouncement in his *Weltraetseln* (World Riddles) that the spirit and soul element – put together as a common term – did not exist as entities in their own right but were only the effects of physiological processes. He regarded psychology as a section of physiology, a view that is still represented today by Anglo-American behaviourism. The French philosopher Lamettrie (1709–51) already propounded in his book *Man – a machine* the theory that the brain exudes thoughts in the same way as the liver exudes gall. Because he gave the body presidence Haeckel called his world-view 'materialistic monism'.

The presentation made by the Nobel Prizewinner John Eccles in 1982[21] to a certain extent conflicts with the Council of Constantinople in 869. In his view it is the self-aware spirit, the human ego, which uses the structures of the brain. Whereas 1115 years ago people tried to separate the spirit from the human soul, John Eccles avoids detaching the concept of soul from that of spirit and calls the conscious self, which he identifies as the soul, the subjective component of the self-aware spirit. This can give us the impression that in the way Eccles describes the reciprocal action of spirit and body a new kind of dualism or dualistic approach is arising, and this is probably because for him the soul element is a consequence of this reciprocal relationship of the spirit with the body in the plane of consciousness lying between them.

This must be the very first occasion in modern times that an attempt has been undertaken in the natural-scientific realm to make a direct study of the self-aware spirit as an active member of the human being, as his actual ego. This must surely be something quite new!

Jesus said: '... The spirit indeed is willing, but the flesh is weak' (Matthew 26:41).[22] The supremacy of the spirit, in the way Eccles sees it, can however lead to overrating the spiritual element and thus disregarding the physical bodily element. Eccles himself, as a natural scientist, ought not to succumb to this revaluation, as the Gnostics were known to have done.[23] Whereas the Gnostics certainly spoke of the presence of God in a human body, that is, of the incarnation of the Logos in the body of Jesus of Nazareth, as in St John's Gospel (Christian Gnosis), they nevertheless were of the opinion that although the Logos had been active on earth it had not actually appeared in the flesh. They spoke of an apparent death, thus denying the resurrection of the body. It was this that prepared the way for the dualism which followed. The spirit does not incarnate in the human body; it enkindles the life of the soul within it, but itself holds back, only guiding it as though from outside. In Haeckel's monism all that was left was a parallelism between the human material part and the spiritual part of the human being, but no actual reciprocal action between them was acknowledged.

Rudolf Steiner also postulated the primacy of the spirit, on account of which he on one occasion called his world conception—in contrast to Haeckel's—spiritual monism. He also laid great stress, however, on the importance of the physical realm, because it is the medium in which the spirit, having become individualized, can know itself and undergo ongoing development. For it is only the capacities we have acquired on earth that can be further developed in the spiritual sphere after death. We are bound to the earth by our bodily nature, and reach up to the heights of heaven in our thinking, so we experience ourselves as human beings only in our discerning feeling and in the feeling quality of our awareness of responsibility. Thus we stand midway between heaven and earth, between spirit world and physical world, between form and matter, as citizens of two worlds. Yet as a self we exist between them in our soul consciousness.

The trichotomy, in its striving for a reciprocal harmonious balance, could be presented thus:

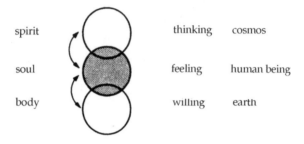

spirit	thinking	cosmos
soul	feeling	human being
body	willing	earth

In our *spiritual nature* we human beings reach in thinking beyond ourselves, but we are also able to take up with us the more exalted experiences we have on earth of the spiritual world (cosmos).

In our *soul nature* we hold the balance between the realm above and the realm below in our feeling consciousness.

In our *bodily nature* we feel ourselves gratefully endebted to the earth. We can pass onto the spirit realm soul fruits acquired whilst living in a body.

All three realms are of equal importance. The earth has to be taken with us; we human beings should not try to escape from it in an irresponsible way for the sake of our own soul salvation. Rudolf Steiner attached great importance to this attitude of shared responsibility.

The evolution of consciousness could be summarized diagrammatically as follows:

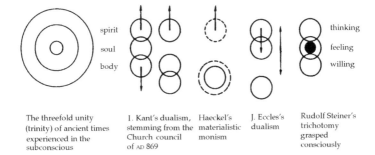

| The threefold unity (trinity) of ancient times experienced in the subconscious | I. Kant's dualism, stemming from the Church council of AD 869 | Haeckel's materialistic monism | J. Eccles's dualism | Rudolf Steiner's trichotomy grasped consciously |

Formerly human beings had knowledge derived from their own spiritual experience. But when this had, in general, faded away, it was replaced by a dogma, a doctrine that people had to believe in (I. Kant); this now applied to the soul realm of the heart. We are led to ask what views and experiences a dogma is based on, especially if it can be altered on the grounds of new attitudes and experiences, as we shall show.

The Aspect of the Soul that Includes Religion

Threefoldness as already presented in Genesis

Most Christians hold that the soul is created by God. But the word soul is often used when people mean spirit. This is understandable because nowadays it is only in the realm of the soul that the spirit can be experienced.

Let me refer to the Greek text of the so-called Septuagint,[24] which I translate as follows:

> And God created [modelled] the human being [*anthropos*] as *dust* of the *earth* and blew the breath, *spirit* [*pneo-en* = *pneuma*] of life [*zoes*] in his face [*prosopon*] and man became a living soul [*eis psykhen zosan*, i.e., psyche, from *psykhē* 'breath, life'].

God as it were breathed a part of his spiritual being into the physical body of man, and soul life arose in him for the first time. When the word 'life' is used it never means vegetative life (*bios*) but always *zoe*, which means spiritual/ soul life.

This also goes to show that in Genesis man was still being considered as a threefold being, consisting of body (dust of the earth) soul (*psykhē*) and spirit (*pneuma*).

When people said that the human soul created by God[25] is added to the foetus only in the last months before birth one wonders where this knowledge comes from. There is nothing about it in the Bible. This assertion is thought to have come from the Greek philosopher Aristotle. It was in all likelihood read into his presentation of life—soul—spirit.[26] What it actually says there is that in the first stage embryos appear to lead a kind of plant life and not until later on is there any question of any apparent soul capable of feeling and, later on still, of any soul life capable of thinking. None of these soul forces could possibly have existed before this. The only alternative would be that just the spirit comes in from outside, and that this alone is divine.

Accordingly, the human soul did not exist before this but only the spirit which has a divine origin. This could mean that the spirit becomes more and more active as it slowly incarnates more and more strongly, gradually awakening the life of the soul. As the spiritual part of the human being works its way in, this would be felt in the movement of the foetus. For soul life engenders movement.[27]

The denial of the direct entry into the human body of the spiritual component of the human being, which was established as a dogma in 869 at the ecumenical Council of Constantinople, brought about a confusion between the concepts of soul and spirit—'soul with some spiritual attributes'. Obviously the first appearance of soul life experienced by the child's movement in the mother's womb was mistaken for the gradual incarnating of the human spirit. This exists of course before conception, and is therefore pre-existent as we have already shown from the memories of mothers, fathers and even children, and more of these will follow.

The ego of the child must, according to this, work in to begin with as though from outside onto the sheath formation (chorion) of the implanted embryo. Around the seventeenth day, however, at the beginning of actual embryonic development, the sudden entering of the ego becomes visible to scientific investigation in the shaping of the embryo when, in the embryonic knot of the blastula, the embryonic disc stretches out and in gathering itself together lengthwise and folding in at the edges lifts itself away from the yolk sac, becoming an entity in itself, separated from its surroundings. This process takes place very quickly within a few hours.

According to Aristotle the level of consciousness of the first stage of embryonic development is plantlike, comparable to our sleep. For as we know from Rudolf Steiner our spiritual ego being withdraws while we are asleep from that part of our nervous system making up the brain and spinal chord, resulting in our no longer having either consciousness or ego-consciousness. The ego—the spiritual core of the human being—remains connected, however, with the vegetative nervous system and at the same time with the body's metabolic organs under its control. As we know, the processes in the metabolic system take place in a plantlike way in the subconscious.

As it was customary, especially in the Dominican Order of the Middle Ages, for people to look to Aristotle when interpreting the Bible or establishing their dogma, and this was the case with Thomas Aquinas (1225–74) among others, it is understandable that they turned to the old Greek view held by Aristotle despite the fact that this view had been misunderstood by the Council of 869. Such conceptions are then able to lead to the opinion that a human being only becomes a human being when he manifests soul stirrings by way of movement. And the earliest moment for this to be possible would not be until the third month of the foetal period onwards or, according to G.L. Flanagan, already in the seventh week after conception.[28]

Admittedly, for some time now the dogma of the Catholic Church that the 'soul' of man created by God is only added to the foetus in the final months before birth has no longer been upheld. Today it is said that the 'soul' is added to the fertilized ovum at the moment of conception. But it will surely be the case, as the history of human consciousness shows us, that many years will have to pass until a true knowledge of these things makes its way into

our basic attitude and from there into the deeper consciousness of humankind.

Is the human being a chance product? St Augustine's theory of predestination

The 'soul created by God' enters a developing bodily
dwelling place which at the moment of conception had
acquired through the genes a particular inherited constitution. According to the view held by materialistic
natural science, the particular combination of inherited
capacities—corresponding to the genetic recombination
that occurs at meiosis[29]—is purely accidental. Thus from
the bodily aspect a human being is a chance product (neo-
Darwinism).[30] So apart from identical twins, the body of
each human being would have a chance selection of different hereditary qualities. Hence according to this view
the 'soul' enters at conception a product that has come
about by sheer chance, and which is delivered to it without
it deserving to have it either for good reasons or bad.

A human being's development is of course influenced
with regard to health and to skills not only by the inherited
tendencies but also by the environmental circumstances
into which he or she is born, and the social implications
these entail. Seen like this they too are accidental conditions
for the particular person as far as the future possibilities
affecting the development of his or her individual personality are concerned. According to this our possibilities
for developing ourselves are dependent on the social
position of the family, national characteristics, place of
birth, language, race, etc., that is, all those conditions which,
according to this view, we are born into involuntarily.

St Augustine (354–430), considered to be the most
prominent Church Father of the West, wondered, among

other things, how it happened that there were believers and unbelievers. As faith, like any other possession, was a gift of God,[31] God must have allotted the good gifts to the one person and withheld them from the other. It was from reflections such as these that his theory of predestination arose. It is the ecclesiastical theory that there is an eternal, inscrutable divine decree whereby a certain number of people are determined by Grace to receive eternal salvation (so-called predestination!) whilst the others are left to a damnation they bring upon themselves. In this case the human being would have had to have the possibility of sinning before he was even born or conceived, or even have damnation predetermined for him (theory of predamnation). Looked at from the human point of view this would be chance, for we would be unable to do anything about the destiny that fell to our lot. Luther rigorously supported the theory of pre-damnation in his document *De servo arbitrio* (i.e. 'slavish verdict'), as did Melanchton in the first edition of *Loci communes rerum theologicarum* (1521), i.e. 'the general fundamental theories of theology'. The English philosopher Henry More (1614–87), whose parents and forefathers were orthodox Calvinists, is said – already as a boy – to have opposed and strongly rejected the harsh predestination theory of Zwingli. Thus Calvin spoke of Grace which was not meted out to everyone but which was nevertheless irresistable and inalienable. Although after Luther's time the Protestant Church distanced itself from this theory just as the Catholic Church had previously done with regard to the ideas of St Augustine, now and again sentiments were expressed in certain ecclesiastical communities of which typical phrases were: 'If a person meets with success, then God is well disposed towards him.' And cases of arrogant behaviour of rich families towards poor folk may have its unrecognized roots in this (see p. 130).

Besides, Augustine formulated the concept of original

sin accordingly: by the Grace of God some of the people lost and damned are saved by Christ without they themselves doing anything towards it. In Islam too, the concept *kismet* (destiny) is based on the theory of predestination.

In short, the theory of predestination has helped pave the way for the coming of Darwinism and the whole subsequent materialistic conception underlying life in today's world—because there is no longer any awareness of an individual ego that carries responsibility.

What is received at conception?

The Church obviously has no proper arguments against the paragraphs on abortion, that is, against abortion altogether. Whose life, whose unborn life is it then, that has to be protected if, after all, the human body in which the 'soul' is destined to live is a chance product? Why should abortion be permitted only when there is either a tendency to illness or to environmental difficulties (social reasons) if, according to the theory of predestination, illness and misfortune(!) are preplanned, according to God's inscrutable decree? Would the mother and the doctor not be acting against the will of God, if . . . ? And what about freedom? In the fundamental law it says in Article 2 paragraph 1 that of course everybody has the right to develop their personality in freedom, but only to the extent that they do not infringe on the rights of others. In this case it is the right of unborn children to have life and to have their bodies constructed, for these will eventually give them the possibility of having human dignity. If from the theological point of view it were also recognized that in the whole process of coming into existence the child is a person right from the beginning, then we should of course want to protect the embryo right from the beginning.

The old word conception points to a receiving, which in earlier times and also today makes one think in the first place not of the receiving of the male sperm but of the 'soul of the child', as it has been called. But where did knowledge of this idea of 'receiving' come from.

A mother reported — and this is confirmed over and over again by other mothers — that intercourse with her husband was a completely different experience on each occasion that resulted in conception. It was different from usual each time. With all her four children she knew exactly when she had conceived a child. She also added that where two of her children were concerned she had an experience like being hurled out into wide spaces. This gives the impression of the being of the mother opening wide for the act of receiving. A young mother described this experience as 'becoming as large as the possibly largest'.[32]

A young woman (as we heard on p. 32) describes the approach to conception of this 'child's soul', the term often used for the ego seeking incarnation. During intercourse with her husband the woman experienced a very bright light coming slowly towards her in a spiral movement. Only later did she realize that the spiral meant that her son was on his way to her.

Another mother reported that when he was a child her son had told her that he was whirled around in a spiral movement on his way to her. And while he spoke he demonstrated these spirals with arm movements. This descent in spirals indicates the way the incarnating process of the child's soul proceeds.[33] This can help us understand why moving in a spiral form is given as therapy in curative eurythmy in cases of weaknesses in the incarnating process, i.e. if a person does not feel that he/she has properly entered into the body during the waking day. You move in a spiral from outside towards the centre — with both arms opened wide and the inner one pointing to the centre (the movement of incarnation). After this the opposite is carried out, moving in a spiral from the centre (the movement of excarnation). This rhythmic interchange between incarnating and excarnating helps one to incarnate better in the body, especially on waking in the morning, so that one comes to oneself quicker and more completely. Children have described this spiral of incarnation; for instance, Renate tells us that on being sent down from heaven she was first of all whirled around the earth before entering 'through the window' into her mother (see pp. 81–2). Also when Angelika announced her arrival the mother-to-be saw a bright light encircling her (see p. 26).

In fact this incarnating spiral appears to be a 'spiritual law of nature'. For it is a well-known fact that with a lot of plants the leaf and bud beginnings of the new twigs grow in a spiral form. Composite flowers like sunflowers (*Helianthus*) show this particularly beautifully in the way the many single blossoms are arranged in a spiral on the flat surface of the flower. Pine and fir cones, too, show us a screw form spiralling up to their tips. It is as though each particular plant, as its plantlike body grows, were gradually incarnating.

So we are becoming aware of a spiritual being which incarnates at conception and follows worldwide laws as it descends in spirals. And there is a powerful force in this incarnating spiritual being. 'The spirit is an onward-driving force.'[34]

Reports from the Bible

How are we to understand the fact that in the Bible the individualities who want to incarnate are announced in a different manner than that among ancient tribes and also in today's society?

In chapter 2, verse 3 of the Tatian Gospel Harmony[35] which originated in the second century, the angel says to Mary: 'Hail, Mary, thou art highly favoured for thou shalt be the mother of God; blessed art thou among women, and blessed is the fruit of thy womb,' and in verse 6 it says: 'The Holy Ghost will come upon Joseph, your promised husband, and the power of the highest shall overshadow thee, O Mary; therefore that holy thing that shall be born of thee shall be called the Son of God . . .' Then in verse 9: 'And on the same day the angel Gabriel appeared to Joseph in a dream, saying: "Hail, Joseph, thou hast been chosen, for thou shalt be the father of God. Blessed art thou among men, and blessed is the fruit of thy loins . . ." ' Furthermore, this choosing of Joseph is described in detail in the Protevangelium of James, 8:2–9:3. Even if we must also take into consideration that in a Gospel Harmony the two varying accounts of the annunciation, in the Gospel of St Matthew and the Gospel of St Luke, appear as it were condensed into one, it nevertheless becomes clear in the way it is presented that in order to enable procreation to take place the divine bidding goes to both partners at the same time. Both Mary and Joseph can now come together intentionally to fulfil a higher command.

A similar account is given in the Protevangelium of James, chapter 1 and 5 of the conception of Anna, who bore Mary, the mother of Jesus.[36] First we are told in detail of the childlessness of the couple Joachim and Anna, who have now grown old. Because of his impotence Joachim loses the right to hold the position of priest and withdraws into the desert, into solitude, in despair. Anna feels doubly punished, in the first place because of the disgrace of being barren, and secondly due to being deserted as a widow. Then the angel of the Lord tells her that she shall conceive and bear a son, and when she has declared herself ready to do this, the angel tells Joachim: 'Go down from here! For see: Your wife will be with child.' The command from on high goes too to both partners, and they know what they have to do.

We also know of the annunciation described in the New Testament (Luke 1:5–25) of the birth of John the Baptist, an annunciation given only to the priest Zacharias, and also of the occurrences narrated in the Old Testament, which led to Isaac being born to Sarah, where the annunciation went directly to Abraham, brought by three archangels no less, while Sarah only listened and laughed, because she was too old (Genesis 17:15–22 and 18:1–16).

Less known is the annunciation of the birth of Samson to the wife of Manoah, as reported in the Old Testament in the Book of Judges 13: 2–5 and 24: 'And there was a certain man of Zorah, of the family of the Danites, whose name was Manoah; and his wife was barren and bare not. And the angel of the Lord appeared unto the woman and said unto her: 'Behold now, thou art barren and bearest not: but thou shalt conceive and bear a son. Now therefore beware, I pray thee, and drink not wine nor strong drink, and eat not any unclean thing. For lo, thou shalt conceive and bear a son; and no razor shall come on his head; for the child shall be a Nazarite unto God from the womb: and he shall begin to deliver Israel out of the hand of the Philistines ... And the woman bare a son, and called his name Samson [Hebrew: little sun].'

It is always archangels who announce the birth or rather

conception and pregnancy. It is like a spiritual bidding being given at that moment to the woman and the man.

Something similar still occurs today but now it is the soul of the child, the individuality, who wants to incarnate, who gives its 'bidding' to the women and to men too. They feel as though they are hearing a call, saying: 'I want to come to you now.' And the cohabitation resulting from this impression is experienced in quite a different way: not as sexual passion but much more reverently, like the sort of cases Hugo Verbrugh quotes. It can help one to feel what is actually meant by the so-called virgin birth. Both in the Gospel of St Matthew and St Luke the father of Jesus, Joseph, is expressly named as the bearer of the Jewish stream of heredity. Thus Mary's virginity must lie solely in her pure state of soul.

So in present times the children's egos announce themselves, whereas in ancient times like that of the Old Testament the announcement of significant personalities was brought by archangels. That children make their own announcements nowadays may indicate that people's individualities have become more independent in keeping with humanity's evolutionary stage of consciousness.

It becomes clear from the testimony we shall be bringing of ancient peoples, and also from biblical accounts which to a large extent coincide with experiences had by present-day mothers and fathers, that we are dealing here with commonly held, ongoing primal experiences. The images often vary to a lesser or greater extent depending on the different level of consciousness in which the experiences come to expression. But we must not allow ourselves to be put off. At the heart of each example we see a kind of fundamental law.

Ancient Tribes Tell their Stories

Members of so-called ethnic tribes are able to say a great deal about prenatal life with regard to the pre-existence of children's souls. Their medicinemen and shamen still have the faculty of supersensible sight such as was possessed by people in the days of cultures long past. It is due to these early forms of consciousness that Richard Karutz, the founder and head of the ethnological museum in Luebeck, calls them prehistoric tribes. I would like to present some accounts of members of these prehistoric tribes. We shall see that their essential content is similar to the kind of experiences that are actually occurring nowadays more and more frequently among our contemporaries.

The Ovambo, a Bantu people in Namibia around the Etosha Pan, closely related to the Herero and the Bergdamara, made dolls called *ounona* children which they take great care of. For instance, if fire breaks out they are the first things to be saved, and they are given later on to the girls when they marry. The doll is looked on as the child of the engaged couple, and the bridegroom gives it a name which is later given to their firstborn. So it is not a toy but is an image of their actual experience of the being who wants to incarnate in the new family, but which still rests in the ancestral spirit, for it is always passed on to the eldest daughter.[37]

The Ewhe negroes in Dahomey say that the soul comes to earth voluntarily from the land of Nodsie. That is, it is his own desire that the spiritual core of his being shall enter into his mother's womb.[38]

Uhtlakanyana, the national hero of the Zulus (Natal and Tongaland in South Africa) said these words in his mother's womb: 'Mother, I am not your child, and your husband is not my father; I was only in your womb, and now go my own way over the earth.'

Here again we have an expression of the human being's own will to live on earth, for which the parents are only the preliminary condition. Accordingly, the child, as a spiritual being, is not the product of his father and mother, something to which they can lay claim.

In the same vein the Arabian writer Kahlil Gibran (1883–1931) in his book *The Prophet, Pointers to a meaningful life* describes a suitable attitude for parents:

> Your children are not your children. They are the sons and daughters of life's longing for itself. They come through you, but not from you. And though they are with you yet they belong not to you. You may give them your love but not your thoughts, for they have their own thoughts...[39]

Richard Karutz writes that with these ancient tribes the individual ego still resides within the spirit of the race and tribe. Therefore when an infant dies among the Ashanti people in Ghana they pray in this way:

> O Mother, who dwell in the land of spirits, we thank you that you allowed this child to come. But we beg you for a new child, and please allow him to stay.

Then the souls will incarnate in the same tribe (see Karutz II, p. 273).

And in Melanje, often before conception, wives hear a voice calling: 'Mother, I am coming to you.'

The natives in eastern Australia say that bronze-coloured middle twigs with orange-coloured blossoms are the transformed souls of children who have clamoured in vain for mothers to incarnate through. The transformation into plants is a picture of the soul remaining in the ether sphere, the moon sphere, where the spirit of the tribe resides. They have to stay there 'lamenting', because they cannot come to birth.[40]

Andrea Lommel who was head of the anthropological institute in Munich, says of the Unambal in Australia that it is the future father who, prior to conception, has the first connection in spirit with the budding souls which are called *Jalala*. A *Jalala*, a child's soul, can appear to him in a dream as a person about the size of a finger. But he only becomes conscious of having found a child's soul when, at the same time, the name of the one who is to come is given him in a dream. In the dream the soul calls out the name containing its being to the man it would like to have for a father.

In the opinion of the natives the dream about finding a child's soul enters in the first place into the heart. The spiritual name then passes from the heart into the head, and the person 'thinks with his head like a wise man'. If, however, someone does not have any soul force in his head, does not have a gift of thinking creatively and formatively, he cannot remember the name the child itself calls out to him. So he cannot take hold of the child's soul either, or pass it onto his wife, which again has to happen in the course of a dream. So a man such as this is not capable of siring children.

All these so-called dream experiences are considered by the Unambal to be absolutely essential for the begetting of a child. According to their view physical procreation alone is not sufficient for producing a child. They are prepared to admit that in the case of white people and also animals this may suffice, but they constantly emphasize that with them a soul disposition is an indispensable part of procreation.

Andreas Lommel thinks that what the Unambal call a 'dream' is what we could call a certain soul disposition, which seems to be a necessary factor for physical potency in the case of peoples whose souls are easily influenced. A child cannot be conceived without preceding dream experiences, however much the parents long for one.

In a case of this kind there is nothing for it but for them to take over from someone else a child's soul that they have found but do not wish to have at the time. This can happen if the 'finder' agrees to such a handing over. They arrange for the transfer, and whilst the one of them dreams in the night of finding a child (i.e. a receptive soul disposition), he 'gives' the child on to the other one.

The finding of a child's soul always happens as though by chance; it cannot be forced or intended. Even people who appear to be gifted in this respect cannot find children's souls on request, but have to wait until they come to them.

The natives also stress the importance of the dream process when the child's soul is handed over to the woman. Physical conception is considered of secondary importance, and only plays a supportive role. They know all about the physical function performed by animals. So it does not appear to be the case, as people often assumed in the past, that the Australian aborigines were ignorant of physiological paternity. It is rather that the natives ascribe to man an exceptional position in nature.[41]

The Unambal can just count to three, and above that there is only 'many'. Yet from among a herd of 10,000 cattle they can distinguish one lost one from all the others by its hoof marks, and thus follow its tracks. They are noted for having a memory that is far beyond our capacity to imagine. In the daytime their consciousness hardly rises above the level of dreams, whereas at night their consciousness hardly sinks at all below the dream level. If they persistently have to work hard for the Europeans they sleep so deeply at night that they cannot remember the name of the future child that is called out to them, and they cannot carry out the handing over of the child in a further dream. This is supposed to be the reason why this race of the Unambal is in the process of dying out.

P. Droste told us that the Australians believe that children arise out of living seeds which come from their ancestors when they wandered over the earth, and that have fallen into the ground at certain places (especially near trees, beside springs and suchlike). Women hurry past these places if they do not want any children. So these tribal peoples know all about the double origin. They are familiar with the physiological process and they also know too that not every cohabitation leads to conception. It is always necessary, but it depends on the human being waiting to be conceived, and who wanders around until it has chosen its parents and can appear to them in a dream.

Biographies

Looking at human biographies it is often quite obvious that there is something like a golden thread, neither intended nor sought for, running through people's lives which remains recognizable despite all deviations and aberrations. It is like a hidden activity through which destiny works, and in which the actual ego reveals itself. People do not experience this 'I' directly in their everyday consciousness but get a glimpse of it on looking back over their lives. Then for the first time they can become conscious of what their actual 'intentions' were, and how they had kept on being diverted from their path by various desires, the need to show off, influences in their environment and world views. A review of their lives can bring clarity regarding the actual plans laid for their path of destiny. Many a poet has tried to solve the life riddles of a famous individual by writing his biography. Goethe tells us in the preface to his theory of colour that people's words, opinions and intentions do not show us what is typical of them: '... If we try in words to describe a person's character our efforts are in vain; whereas if we line up their actions, their deeds, then a *picture* of their character will appear before us.'

So a person's real being retreats before an externally defined approach, and can be experienced to start with only in picture form.

Thus those impressive dreams or visions mothers can have before or after their child is conceived are pictures of the coming human being and their intentions in life. For we were given many reports which referred to the character and disposition of the coming child. The mother can learn something of the way in which the child will enter into its environment. In the background of the experiences a mother had, her son was able to convey to her the plans he later took up in his work in agriculture and in the protection of the threatened environment.

The following descriptions of dreams are particularly striking pictures of the coming child's later field of professional activity.

Mrs A.: The first dream with my third child comes at the end of the third week after conception. This time I was standing by myself at the open window of the room that was my bedroom at the time. It was night-time and yet the radiant sun shone high in the sky between the west and the North Star, where it is normally never seen. I fixed my eyes on it, for I noticed that it was constantly changing. I remember that it took on a dark shade of red, blue and violet, and that the earth suddenly shook and I was afraid. Then I heard myself saying: 'It is of course Good Friday.' And so saying I woke up. It really was the night between Maundy Thursday and Good Friday (I had certainly been thinking earlier on about the tragic events of these days, but only about the crucifixion and the laying in the grave, not at all about the eclipse of the sun and the earthquake). To start with I never thought of a child. About a week later I felt the first symptoms of pregnancy. A little later on I dreamt that I was sitting paralysed at the open window of our nursery looking down at the meadow and the surrounding hedge. I saw behind the hedge a child of two to three years dressed all in white walking along holding the hand of a friend of mine. In the meadow there was a circular pond which does not exist in reality. The sun was reflected in this pond and coloured the water purple. Filled with joy of having seen my child I could rise from the chair, and I leapt joyfully into the pond, right into the sun. (Without knowing about my dream my friend asked me later whether she could be godmother.)

This son is particularly concerned about the suffering in the world and takes it very much to heart, but he tries to help through his profession as a curative teacher.

Mrs A.: When I was pregnant with my sixth child, a boy again, whom we were not expecting at all, I had an intense dream experience but I cannot give any actual details. It was simply overwhelming, because of the mood it brought with it. There was indescribable pain at first, and deep sadness passing gradually over into indescribably beautiful coloured light, music and tremendous joy. I hesitated to begin with to interpret this dream experience as a sign of pregnancy, but a little while later I noticed that it happened again to be at the end of the third week after conception.

Just a few weeks later, after my condition had been confirmed, I had a very simple, intimate dream. A boy about nine or ten years old appeared from out of a dark green pine forest. He walked towards me, but then turned left, in the direction of the house where I was born, for the forest was clearly that of my childhood. In his hand the apparently happy little fellow carried a small Christmas tree decorated and covered with lighted candles.

Even when he was only in class I there was nothing our youngster enjoyed more than going into the forest by himself at 5 o'clock in the morning to watch the animals and the birds and to bring home to his mother rare and beautiful things. Later on, during his apprenticeship as a forest warden he was regularly allowed to fell our Christmas tree himself, which he carried home to decorate together with one of his brothers.

Through experiences such as these, beginning right from the annunciation of the child, an openness is being prepared in the parents towards the unfolding of their child's intentions. To what extent the child's right development depends on the parents and the wider environment is something we usually know very well from our own experiences or those of our immediate surroundings. This aspect will be followed up in later contributions.

So a child in its mother's womb already feels stirring of will such as certain interests and intentions which it will endeavour to realize at some time on earth, and which it conveys to its mother in this way. Are hidden indications such as these also to be seen in the biographies of children and young people? We will look for things like this in the following biographical sketches.

The explosion in the barn

When a six-year-old boy did his first experiment in physics it ended in an explosion. The barn went up in flames. Black with soot, it was only with the greatest effort that he made his way out. 'Branded' as an arsonist—and he did have blisters—he was publicly beaten like a thief in front of the vicar, the teacher and the mayor of the small town of Milan (in Ohio, USA) and he suffered greatly from the shame of it. When the frail little boy was seven years old his father took his family to Port Huron, 200 km away, where he then sold groceries and wood. He set up a little laboratory for his son in the cellar of his house. His mother lived in constant fear that the house might be blown up any day. Tom, as the boy was called, only went to school for three months, after which his mother taught him. When he was twelve he became a 'train boy' selling fruit and refreshments in the trains of the Michigan North-South Railway. But he kept on doing experiments, in fact he did so every spare moment. He rigged himself up a printing press in the luggage van, listened to the travellers' accounts from the battle zones, and printed his own paper, distributing it himself. Did he know why he did these things? Was it not as though there was an irresistible urge in him to be technologically active? A lot of children do experiments, of course, but do they stick to it? Tom had a favourable destiny in that he had a father who had understanding for his son's drive to do experiments. In the course of his life Tom acquired 2500 patents, invented the light bulb, the gramophone and much, much more. He was Thomas Alva Edison (1847–1931).

The trans-Siberian railway

When, in 1912, work was begun on building the railway line via Irkutsk to the Far East the father of little Michail was sent from St Petersburg to be a doctor at a building site near Irkutsk. Michail was five years old and could not go to school because it was too far away. So he roamed around the neighbourhood, far and near, collecting bones, stuffing animal skins and exhibiting them in a barn. When he was ten he began systematically to do excavations. In a school essay, in answer to the question 'What do you want to become?', he wrote at the time that he wanted to be an archaeologist and model the structure of living creatures from seeing their bones—not animals but early man.

When he was 13 he became an active member of the local topography institute, attending school in the morning and the local university, sitting among students, in the afternoon. When he was 13 he made his first experiment with skulls. He asked Professor Grigoriev whether he thought it would be feasible to make an authentic reconstruction of the face on the skull of a person belonging to the present. His answer was: 'Indeed, colleague, I am convinced that is possible . . .' even though he knew himself that up till then every attempt in this direction had miscarried. Many years of intensive work followed, watched with mistrust and envy by his older colleagues, until finally Michail succeeded in developing the right method. In 1963 he was invited to go to Weimar to establish whether the skull Goethe found in 1826 of Friedrich Schiller who had died in 1805 was the genuine article, which people continued to doubt. By putting an authentic reconstruction of his face onto the skull he was indeed able to supply proof of its authenticity.

If the building of the trans-Siberian railway had not been started in 1912 Michail Michailovitch Gerassimov (born 1907) would have had to stay in St Petersburg. He would have attended the grammar school without being able to come in touch with bone findings which were particularly numerous in the region of Irkutsk. It was ordained by his own destiny, as we say, because he himself wanted it. And he was supported too by the right teachers. He just had to know, without being put off, what he wanted — and he knew this from the age of ten — and this was to continue what he had been practising doing, subconsciously, dreamily, instinctively, since the age of five.

Artist or zoologist

Six-year-old Adolf's father, who was a rough labourer in Basle, had to supply his son with books from which he could copy pictures of animals. He found the colourful birds and their feathers particularly enthralling. During his training as an artist he later on came in touch at the university with zoology, and his enthusiasm was kindled for animals and animal behaviour. For almost 40 years he was head of the zoological institute in Basle and developed it further. He gave a lot of lectures which were very popular, and his descriptions, especially of animal forms, brought it home to people that he had acquired the gift of observation by drawing as a child. If you want to be a master you have to start practising early, but in his case he was not a master of painting but of description. He was Adolf Portman (1897–1982). When he was six years old he was driven to drawing and painting. Did he know why he was driven to it?

From bookbinding apprentice to physicist

Michael was the third son of a blacksmith's assistant in a village near London. He had four years of the sort of schooling available in those days, after which he delivered newspapers and books for a bookseller. He finally became an apprentice to a bookbinder who specialized in binding university books. Luckily for Michael there was not much to do, so he had the time to spare to read the books that were being bound. He then participated in evening courses in physics, repeated in the most primitive fashion the experiments which were demonstrated, and wrote detailed procedural reports about them. After a seven-year apprenticeship he became a junior partner to another bookbinder who had no sympathy for the fact that he also read the books he bound. Michael packed up his manuscripts together with his notes and the reports of his experiments he had made on the strength of his evening courses, and sent them to his professor. The latter said to his assistant: 'If he is content to wash the glasses he is someone, if he is not then he is useless.' The professor was amazed to watch the way Michael washed the glasses: carefully, conscientiously, actually lovingly. Michael soon had to prepare the experiments, then demonstrate them to the students, whilst the professor gave his lecture. Finally he was entrusted with the care of the laboratory, and he accompanied the professor on his European travels, where he made the acquaintance of many famous specialists. When the professor died Michael became his successor. This significant physicist of the nineteenth century was Michael Faraday (1791–1867). Did Michael the book-binding apprentice know what drove him to read the university books? He was also apprenticed to the one who was the right instructor for him. Although he was not conscious of it, of course, he chose well! But it was the ego force of his own will that had to supply the drive to work enormously hard. Destiny only creates the opportunity.

The whole house collapsed

When his master's house collapsed Joseph came out of the wreckage unhurt. The King of Bavaria, King Max, heard about this, and because Joseph had been sent at the age of twelve to be an apprentice to a mirror manufacturer and glass cutter, King Max gave him the wherewithal to acquire his own glass cutting machine. The court councillor v. Utzschneider asked him what else he would most like to have, and the 14-year-old asked for books on physics and mathematics. When he was 20 he became an assistant in an institute of mathematics and mechanics, where he made the best glass lenses and knew how to follow this up with the most exact of calculations and skilful cutting. It was he who cut the largest lens of his time for an astronomical telescope. He discovered in the solar spectrum the lines called after him, became a professor at the age of 36, and was then knighted for his great scientific achievements. Joseph von Fraunhofer (1787–1826) died at the early age of 39.

Would he ever have had the chance to benefit from the effect of what led him to a scientific career such as this if people's attention had not been drawn to the poor glazier's apprentice through the 'lucky' accident? This was the way destiny helped him, but only in his particular case; for he evidently — without actually knowing this of course — had wanted to become something other than a glazier like his father, whose tenth child he was. He had requested to have books on mathematics and physics, for his impulse drove him in that direction, although he had only had four years elementary education. He brought with him a talent which was hidden to start with, and this enabled him to gain the required knowledge quickly. In his optical work he was ceaselessly active, allowed himself no rest or recuperation, and actually died of not recovering properly from pneumonia. As his biographer E. Lommel writes, the hidden capacities he brought with him were 'profound ingenuity, a tremendous power of invention, untiring perseverance, a strong love of truth and technical mastery'.

Going against the stream

When Florence Nightingale was still a child she and her mother and father were passing one day through the poor quarter of London. Florence asked with horror: 'Do these people have to be so poor?' And her mother replied arrogantly: 'You do not need to concern yourself about these people, Florence. God happens to have made rich and poor people. And He will know why He arranged it that way and not another way. It is by no means *our* task to overturn His order of creation.' She noticed Florence frowning, so she continued emphatically: 'You should thank the good Lord that you are not in the same state as these poor people!' Florence was of course grateful, but at the sight of that poverty she felt sad. Already as a small child she was different from other children; playing bored her, so she learnt early to read and write, worked at her school books, and because she had nobody to talk to who understood her she wrote diaries (in fact she did this all her life). She wanted eventually to be a nurse, that is, take up a profession which in England at the end of the nineteenth century belonged among the most despised of professions. Almost nobody in their circle of friends understood her, as her parents were very rich and were much respected in society. It was a thorny path for this young woman who in the meantime had risen to become matron of a dilapidated Home for Ladies. When in 1854 the Crimean War broke out she organized, at the age of 34, voluntary nursing in Scutari, in the vicinity of Istanbul/Constantinople, and then in the Crimea at Balaclava on the outskirts of Sebastopol. The soldiers honoured her with the special name of 'the angel with the lamp' which she carried when she groped her way at night through the rows of wounded and dying, bringing them help and comfort. She gave her whole inheritance, a large fortune, to pay for the necessary equipment. At the end of her life, after she had trained many nurses and sent them to many countries, with the help of a donation from Queen Victoria she was able to found a school for district nurses, which had been her last wish. She died in 1910 at the age of 90.

Why did Florence Nightingale take this difficult path in life, one which she pursued with an energy and force that stopped at nothing, fighting as a woman against a man's world, asserting herself against doctors and officials, just as she had resisted tradition and custom as a child? Right from the beginning she had to fight her own way through every hindrance. Help never came by itself; she had to ask for it, beg for it, unerringly following a path set her — not by her own needs but by those of her environment. What strength there must have been in her to fight her way free despite everything the parental home offered to spoil and tempt her. The sight of such need awoke in her the impulse she had brought into life, so that she was able to carry out consciously what she had evidently brought with her.

Yet certain physical prerequisites were necessary, such as for instance her philanthropic father's extensive circle of acquaintenances, giving Florence the chance to get near these influential personalities. And the element which tore her out of English family tradition had to be pre-planned! The child was born in Florence during the Nightingale's honeymoon trip, and because her parents did not know what they should call her they simply called her after her birthplace, Florence. We can already detect in this a certain lack of inner connection between mother and child, and later on the girl always felt inwardly alienated from an English environmental setting. This made her independent at an early age. At the hour of her birth the stars over Florence were of course differently placed than they would have been over London! Florence had chosen this, and so to say encouraged her parents to travel through Florence on their honeymoon. Earthly and cosmic constellations have to work together to form such a unique destiny. And that she was born as a woman and not a man was very important for this individuality (the spiritual core of a human being is of course in itself not affected by sex) because only in a female body was it possible to feel such strong compassion and sympathy and to have the readiness to make sacrifices. She also specially needed to have a high level of intellectuality, which she inherited from her father's side. The latter quality helped Florence not to lose control over her feelings, but always to apply discretion. What motivated her was willingness to make sacrifices, not self-sacrifice, because she never acted egoistically, but with a selfless eye to what, as she herself put it, God expected of her.

With these few more or less well-known examples we wanted to draw special attention to the way a person's ego being, out of its conscious knowledge of its destiny and the will to carry out particular deeds, can be seen in childhood driving the child, albeit unconsciously, in the direction it needs to take.

Repeated Earth Lives

There were a number of clear pointers in the first part of this book coming from experiences which suggest that human beings are born more than once. Over and above this there are numerous reports giving very precise details of a knowledge of past earthly lives. By comparing many such accounts we can recognize relatively easily whether the statements could be true, as we get an impression of a regular pattern.

Although it does not belong to the actual theme of this book to give lengthy accounts of experiences of repeated earth lives, our presentation of prenatal life from the point of view of the pre-existence of the spiritual core of a human being would however remain unsatisfying if we did not also bring a few thoughts about the deeper meaning of people's life aims and talents and the blows of destiny and illnesses they suffer. For the idea of reincarnation includes that of the pre-existence of the human being. We are therefore going to bring a few examples pointing to a knowledge of these facts.

Statements from ancient tribes

So let us again bring some views on life handed down to us from early tribes. We shall be looking back from our present-day self-aware but spiritually poverty-stricken civilization to an ancient mentality still in a state of child-like, dreamy spirit closeness, which can suggest to us the path of development of humankind altogether.

Australian: After departing from the body the soul flies around as *njer*, enters into an animal as *rai*, after which it is fit to be born again.

Eskimo: After death the human soul enters the kingdom of the seals.

From the Arctic: The soul enters into a series of animals but leaves each time voluntarily because it does not feel at ease there, and the animal then dies, the soul moving on to enter finally into a woman.

The image of the animal signifies the realm of soul and of instinct which governs existence in the moon sphere between the earth and the moon and in which dwell the group souls of the animal species as well as the spirits of the tribes and races of the native peoples.

When human beings die the spiritual core of their being leaves the physical body. When it says that the animal dies when the human soul moves on, what it means is that the human individuality leaves the 'body' of the animal group soul. It can only mean a spiritual body of the animal group. The human being 'dies' in the spiritual world when he entrusts himself to his parents to be born on earth.

When, as the inhabitant of the Arctic says, the soul 'is not at ease in the animals', this must be referring to the experience in purgatory, the realm of soul purification, Kamaloka.[42] After death the human being gradually sloughs off the animal quality of his instinctive nature, and leaves it behind as a skin so that it can gradually dissolve — the 'animal' in him now dies, after the physical body was left behind on earth to be dissolved.

In oriental countries people have spoken since olden times of the migration of the soul, and we constantly hear of the idea that a rebirth could occur not only in a human body but also in an animal, and this is so in the Hindu belief even today.[43]

The view of reincarnation of the spiritual core of the human being that has been promoted by adherents of German spiritual life since the dawn of their classical period does not mean that human beings can reincarnate in the body of an animal or even that it dwells in one temporarily. Not even the ancient Indian sages ever considered that soul migration included passing through the physical body of animals, because they knew that progressing as a human being meant the overcoming of animal nature. However, when clairvoyance disappeared — and this actually happened in the Orient first — the tradition was misunderstood, and in Hinduism people have imagined till this day that reincarnation takes place in animal bodies. This misunderstanding does not occur among early tribes, because their shamen — medicine men — still possess genuine clairvoyance.

An Ewhe Negro of the Dahomey tribe greets the child as an ancestor who has become a living human being again, and asks it how things stand in the spirit world. He is of course not bearing in mind that before the soul enters incarnation it has to forget its experiences as a spirit so as to have the chance of being a free human being.[44]

A Negro once imagined that he was his own grandfather who was reborn in him.

Besides, the German word for grandchild, *Enkel*, means little ancestor, little grandfather. Not only among the Germanic tribes but also among many of the ancient tribes, especially the early ones, we find innumerable references to the view that the grandfather or an ancestor of the tribe reincarnates in grandchildren. Apparently this happens as a rule only within the tribe.[45]

The Ashanti (Ghana) comes again in the same maternal tribe and the same paternal *ntoro*, in a circle of spiritual relationships out of which the child's name is given.

The Native Americans kept certain names as a family possession and gave them to a child in whom the clairvoyant priest doctor had foreseen the qualities and capacities of a particular ancestor.

The Kamba (East Africa) say that if a baby cries a lot and refuses the breast the reincarnated ancestor within it is restless because the child has not yet been given its name, i.e. it has not yet been recognized in the child. He exhorts the parents in a dream to 'call him by his rightful name'.

Nomen est omen — the name is also a prediction.[46] The Latin word *omen* is related to the Greek word *oiomai* = I foresee, I anticipate. This corresponds to the Middle High German expression *mich anet* meaning as good as 'it comes to me'. The concept of foreseeing points to an experience which in medieval times was felt to be a kind of 'being overshadowed by a spiritual being of which one could have a presentiment'. It was in this way that the approaching ancestor could be experienced. Names were once upon a time experienced as a manifestation of a person's being, as the meaning of many names shows us. People still 'saw' the destiny and life task of the incarnating individuality and named the child accordingly. You may dwell quietly on the idea — without looking for an immediate intellectual answer — of what a child's soul is intimating when it tells its mother, even before its conception, the name it wants to be called by.[47] It is also extremely important that we call a child by its Christian name, so that it can be called into its growing body. If it is just called 'Baby' or 'Pet' or something like that, experience shows that it becomes more difficult for the 'I' to incarnate as a spiritual being in the body, and a lack of self-awareness can result.

We can gather from the reports of early tribes that these are based on clairvoyant perceptions of the medicine men and shamen who are able to accompany the human beings after death. They describe how the soul passes through the realm of the spirit of the tribe or race where also live the group souls—actually the group egos—of the various animal species who as it were partly incorporate themselves (not incarnate) in the particular animals they belong to. They only partly enter into the bodily sheaths. The human soul feels related to these different animal soul beings in accordance with the kind of soul qualities that predominate in its own soul make-up. This realm of the souls of the tribes and races is however evidently full of etheric formative forces. The Baya Negroes (formerly a culturally high-ranking Sudanese tribe south of the Chad) calls the sphere of life forces *gbasso* = great spirit = spiritual world, in which the soul lives until it has grown old and dies, to be born anew on earth.[48]

This sphere of the etheric formative forces is where the human being goes first after death. According to the early tribes they remain there journeying on under the influence of the spirit of the tribe until, as the Ibo Negroes (in the Niger delta) say, they see the souls of the children coming down out of the world of the trees or, as the Busingo Negroes (on the Kasai, the southern part of the Congo) say, the souls descend to earth out of the sacred trees, referring to the sphere of the etheric formative forces out of which the soul/spiritual part of the human being descends again. If a Negro has become powerful, rich and respected in life, however, he is not born again. For the shaman cannot find him any more in the realm of the tribal spirit after death, as he is so to say lost to his clairvoyant sight. Each individual incarnates in his tribe with the approval of the spirit of his ancestors (the group soul of his tribe) until he has fulfilled the task set him—that is, until his ego being disengages itself from the group soul and his destiny separates from the tribal group.

The ethnologist Guenther Tessmann travelled in particular in the areas around the South Cameroons and the

Bay of Douala. When he asked the Bubi on the Fernando Po about the customs there they turned the question round on him and asked him whether he had forgotten everything, because as their old chief he was the best person to know about it!

If we refer back to the previous indications about the human being's path between death and a new birth (pp. 137–8) we can say that the individuality extricating itself from the sphere of influence of the tribal spirit was moving on from the moon sphere to the sun sphere, and therefore was no longer perceptible to the medicine man. The individual who has progressed now goes on the long journey through the varied world of spiritland, and it often takes centuries until it returns to earth, now among a different people, however, and is born into a more highly developed race that offers further possibilities of development. According to this, Tessmann felt himself drawn to the place where he had been active in past lives, and the Negroes could obviously have at least an inspired feeling for the truth. With regard to the two possible ways of reincarnating Hans-Hasso von Veltheim-Ostrau wrote:

> So we must allow for there being two aspects of rebirth in general, in that we distinguish for instance between reincarnation and soul migration. We then come to the conclusion that people who are of a group soul nature pass through soul migrations and incarnate again fairly rapidly after death, whereas individuals — meaning people who are consciously going through ego development — reincarnate, which is something that is characterized by considerably longer spells of time between death and a new birth.[49]

Children who die early can also come back quickly. In this connection we are told that the Rilke family had a daughter first, called Maria, but she died young. After her

came a son of whom the mother maintained that it was
Maria being born again. Hence the name Maria Renée
(Maria, the reborn one) which, translated into German was
Rainer Maria, Rainer being the German version of Renée.[50]
A woman told us that after having several children she
finally gave birth to a daughter who, however, died of an
illness in her fifth year. Many years later she had another
child, also a girl. Once, when she was revisiting the
cemetary and wept at the grave of her dead daughter, the
child who was born later on said to her mother: 'You do not
need to cry any more, because I have come back! I still
remember clearly how you laid me to rest here, for I had
been very ill.'

We could leave the question open as to whether in the
case of children who return quickly it is a matter of
reincarnation or only migration of the soul in the above
sense, because they are born again so soon and in the same
families.[51] But apart from the fact that I at least am not
familiar with a tribal spirit in the case of the white race that
would compare with what has been said of the coloured
races, the possibility of a quick return can be explained
otherwise. In the existence between death and a new birth
a child has neither acquired much in the way of accumu-
lated destiny to transform in the realm of purification nor
has it brought from its life on earth very much of significance in the way of acquired capacities needing to be
worked on. Therefore it can pass rapidly through the soul
and spirit realms and return soon. But the experience
gained by illness could be the kind of thing which is
important for a later incarnation, and the soul can enter a
new life with greater strength.

It is easy to see that people who have only had a short
soul journey or who only dwell in the spiritual world for a
short time between death and a new birth can still
remember their previous incarnation. In fact even the

bodies of the following incarnations are similar. Here are just a few examples of this.

Experiences among members of the white race

That an obviously very recent incarnation can have the effect of making the facial features of the body actually similar is shown in the following example.[52]

An Englishman whose name was F. Moss gave this account. 'In 1919 I went to Germany with the occupying forces. Soon after my arrival in Cologne I felt strangely at home in the neighbourhood. Following up this feeling of being at home I went with a few of my comrades to the wonderful Cologne Cathedral. Before entering I gave them an exact description of the interior of the Cathedral, which I had never seen in this life — yet knew so well. And there is more. With a couple of pals I went by local railway to a place called Engelskirchen, a few km from Cologne. When we got there I told my pals that there must be a place called Freilingsdorf close by. Again my words proved correct. But the greatest surprise of all was the look of amazement on the face of the old innkeeper in Freilingsdorf who immediately ran off to fetch an old portrait — dated 1756 — showing a boy in the national costume of the eighteenth century whose facial features were so similar to mine in every detail that one could not say they were similar but only that they were totally identical.'

A further example of an exact recollection:[53]
'A boy drew a picture of a round Negro hut with a peculiar outlet for smoke ... In front of the hut he drew a naked woman with long, hanging breasts. Beside the hut there was water with waves and palm trees in the back-

ground. He then showed the picture to me, his mother, and explained: We lived in huts like these, we made them ourselves. Just as everyone made a boat for himself by hollowing out a tree-trunk and carving it. There was a wide river there, but we could not go down deep into it because some kind of monster lived in the water which bit off people's legs... Now you know why I yelled the whole time last year when you wanted to take me into the water. And do you remember, Mummy, when we bought a big boat last year I wanted to row straight away. I knew that I can row... Look, here I am standing and hunting a large bird, and my hat is lying beside me. His mother asked him: Why did you draw your wife with such long, hanging ugly breasts?... Because that is what they were like! And that is not ugly! She was very beautiful! he added proudly... Later on, when he was 15 years old, he asked me to buy him a large jazz drum... He took two drumsticks, sat down beside her and immediately beat out the most difficult rhythms and impossible syncopations with great skill, as though it was the most natural thing in the world. He drummed ecstatically, his eyes radiant, and tears running down his cheeks... While playing a very strange rhythm he said: You see, Mummy, this is how we sent one another various signs and messages over tremendous distances, and he drummed away like someone possessed.'

Much later on, when Paul Brunton[54] visited the family, his mother, Mrs E. Haich, showed him her son's drawings. To which he said: This style of hut is typical of a Negro tribe in Central Africa on the banks of the Zambezi. He has drawn it correctly in every detail. And the 'modern felt hat' is woven from reeds and is typical of that tribe. Even his hunting knife is drawn correctly. And the monster that bites legs off is of course a crocodile! There are lots of crocodiles there...

As we have already given one example (p. 47) of a ten-year-old boy playing at 'farmyards' with a girl who remembered them and knew all the details better then the teacher, let us mention the following with reference to a past memory.

Mrs Haich's son never wanted to read Negro stories. Why should I? After all, I know better what it was like there than they do. Why do I need to know what white people think of it? And when I read proper descriptions I always have to weep, whether I want to or not... Later on, when he was a flying officer, he saw a Negro film with his mother. The overgrown boy cried in the dark like a child; he sobbed, and could not stop the tears running down his cheeks.[55]

When we think about reports like these we can understand some of the strange, spontaneous things that occur with our own children.

The following account could also point to a recent incarnation. It is from the life story of — let us call her — an Egyptian American lady.[56]

She was the only child of respected and well-off American parents. Photos taken when she was two, three, four years of age show a serious face with a touch of unchildlike wisdom. Her parents and grandparents did all they could to accustom the child to speak English. But she stubbornly persisted in expressing everything in a language of her own. When they pressed the child to say table or chair she was enraged, and refused impatiently to repeat the words said to her, replacing them with other words which nobody understood. This strange behaviour made such an impression on her mother that she eventually recorded in a book every single word and phrase the child said and put the English meaning beside it... Meanwhile the nine-year-old girl was eventually taken to a sympathetic psychiatrist whom she could tell all about it. The doctor gave her the following explanation.

'There is nothing wrong with you. I understand you fully and completely — and one day the others will understand all that you have told me. But they cannot understand it at present, and whilst this is so your behaviour understandably worries your parents. Promise me that you will now forget everything you have told me — the foreign language you speak and all the places and events you can recollect so well, and for the time being let them rest and think only of doing everything your parents want you to do. For all they want is for you to be well, sensible and happy ... Forget everything that has happened and see and learn only what there is to learn in *this* life!'

The girl promised and never broke her word. When she attended the university she showed an unusually good grasp of the history of antiquity and the philosophy and religions of the East, as though she had been familiar with them for a long time.

At the age of 45 she and her husband stayed in Egypt as the guests of a well-known Arab leader. At the banquet in honour of his American guests the Arab told her that his mother wanted to show her a jewelry box containing precious stones which were thousands of years old and were inherited from an ancestor, a great queen.

'My mother will speak French with you, Madame, so that you will understand each other well,' said the Arab. 'With her servant, however, she speaks a language so old that we do not even know its name. The servant's ancestors have of course served in this house for millennia.'

She was then led to the host's mother's apartments, who asked the servant in a strange language to fetch the queen's jewels. The servant seemed shocked at this request and humbly reminded her mistress that these treasures had never yet been shown before the eyes of foreigners. At these words the American lady raised her hand and said in French: 'Say no more about it; I understand every word you and your servant are saying!'

Horrified and ashamed, the old lady sent for her son who apologized for the tactlessness. 'But it seems to make no sense in the face of the fact that you, Madame, understand the language of our ancestors! Is it possible? Where did you learn it?'

'Not in this life,' the American lady replied, 'but I was born knowing it, and I have tormented my parents enough with it, wanting to speak only that language for years. I have not given any thought to it for many years now, but when your mother conversed in this language the whole memory came alive in me again.'

Her host then begged her urgently to send to America for the book in which her mother had written down the words and phrases. When the Arab had had a look at it he was shaken and said: 'For one or another karmic reason, or in order to learn something from it, your previous life occurred in our tribe. That much is now clear to me.'

From then on unusual trust was placed in the American lady, for the Arabs looked on her as one of their own.

Ancient oriental views

As Muslims Arabs do not believe in reincarnation. However, in ancient Sufism (Islamic mysticism), which originated in the second century of Hedshra, which is AD 800, the Sufi Dshelal ud Din Rumi (Dshelaledin Rumi, 1207–73) sings the praises of the idea of reincarnation as follows:

> I died as plant and returned as animal. After innumerable lives I died from the animal realm and became a human being. So why be afraid? Have I become any less through dying? Next time I shall die from the human

realm to grow angel's wings. And leaving the angels behind me I will become what surpasses all imagining. Then let me enter into God. Are not the strings of my harp calling to me: Truly, to Him, to God, we all return.[57]

Sufism taught that the human spirit was an emanation of the Divine and aspired to reunite with the Divine.[58]

We could presume that the Arab leader in Egypt knew something about Sufism, for the Sufi conception of reincarnation seems to be more widespread among Muslims than is commonly supposed—a comfort, perhaps, compared to the religious belief of kismet.[59]

Jewish legends,[60] too, tell us the following about reincarnation. At the end of the 40 years sojourn in the desert and after the death of Moses, Joshua (from the tribe of Ephraim) took over the leadership of the children of Israel. Before he crossed the Jordan he sent two spies to Jericho,[61] and Rahab took them in at her inn. This is recounted in the Book of Joshua in the Old Testament immediately following the five Books of Moses.

The Jewish legends also include the following account. Rahab—one of the four most beautiful women who have ever lived—became a Jewess and married Joshua. In Joshua, the son of Nun, Joseph, the son of Jacob, was reborn (Joseph was of course sold into Egypt). And because Joseph had been hesitant to take the wife of his master Potiphar, the Pharoah's chief court councillor, Joshua had to marry Rahab in whom the Egyptian woman had been reborn.

So Joseph, the son of Jacob, who was sold into Egypt in 1890 BC reincarnated as Joshua (1260–1170), i.e. about 700 years later, and Potiphar's wife (born about 1900 BC) was reincarnated as Rahab, the innkeeper of Jericho. In this example from the Old Testament we also see something of the way destiny, karma, works. And in the Talmud

(Hebrew for instruction), in the law orally passed down from ancient times, and written down in the first centuries after Christ, it says that at the time of Christ the Jews more or less generally believed in the migration of souls. The Talmudists presumed that God had only created a certain number of Jewish souls, and therefore they returned again and again as long as Jews existed, being sometimes transferred in punishment into the body of an animal. But on the Day of the Resurrection they would all be purified and come to life again in the bodies of the Just in the Promised Land.[62]

Also among the ancient civilized races people still knew of reincarnation. For instance in Egypt, whilst the royal Prince Herutataf was visiting a temple, he found at the feet of the statue of a god a chapter of the Egyptian Book of the Dead which dates back to the reign of King Men-Kau-Ra, i.e., *c.* 2700 BC.[63] This chapter begins with the words:

I am Today.
I am Yesterday.
I am Tomorrow.
Moving through repeated births I remain strong and
    young...
See, I fly like a bird,
And floating in the air I descend to earth...
Stepping forth I follow the tracks
of my previous deeds; for I am
A child of Yesterday,
My becoming is in the keeping of the gods of Akeru.

In the Indian *Bhagavadgita* it says:

If our clothes are worn out
    we put aside our old ones,
And in their place
    we put on new ones.

In old age we rest
   after life's exhausting struggle,
Leaving in the grave
   the earthly garment of our body.
Until nature has once again
   made us a bodily sheath,
A new garment,
   lovingly prepared in our mother's womb.
And when we awaken again,
   there shines in golden splendour
The youthfully radiant day,
   which arose before us as a miracle.

The concept of reincarnation in fairy tales and legends

Time and again we find the idea of repeated earth lives appearing in popular fairy tales and legends. Here are just a few examples.

The best known fairy tale about reincarnation is the story of 'Mother Holle' and the two daughters. It is worth noticing that the individuality who in her next incarnation returns to earth through the gate of birth as the ill-fated girl was described as having been 'ugly and lazy' in her previous incarnation. It appears that through the forces of atavistic consciousness in her natural mother who, however, was already a 'widow'[64] she is still favourably treated. There was no need for her to work hard in her earthly life to acquire the forces of a new consciousness as the stepdaughter has to do. The latter developed wakeful thought forces, in the image of spinning 'threads of thought', though she had to acquire these by making a sacrifice and renouncing old heart forces. She was 'beautiful and industrious', and also kind, for she took all the bread out of the oven, shook all the apples down from the tree and carried out the tasks set her by Mother Holle as willingly as she had always served her stepmother throughout earthly life. She took willingness, diligence and kindness into the spiritual world with her. Together with the newly acquired thought forces she was also given spiritual gold on her way through the gate to her new earthly life. The lazy one, on the other hand, brought with her the conditions to be born with negative qualities, on the basis of which she always has bad luck in life. The bad luck or, according to the other meaning of the German word *Pech*, the pitch stuck fast to her and could not be shaken off as long as she lived. That Mother Holle's house means the spiritual world comes out very expressively when we are told that golden Mary, despite the fact that she was so well off in the spiritual world, feels a longing to 'go home', i.e. to the earthly world where she will be able to acquire new capacities. As we saw, the human being's spirit/soul being longs for a new life on earth.

Gotthold Ephraim Lessing, German philosopher and educationalist, speaks about this already in his *Education of the Human Race*: Why should I not return as many times as I am capable of acquiring new knowledge and abilities?

We can put it another way and say that we wait in the spiritual world until earth conditions have developed to the extent that there are new things for us to learn. Or it might also be the case that it is when the world situation requires it, and we can play our part anew in world evolution with our faculties which have by then sufficiently matured. This last aspect is touched on in the Kyffhäuser legend of Emperor Friedrich Barbarossa (1152– 90) who is asleep within his mountain fortress awaiting the restoration of the unity of the German people. In Friedrich Rueckert's (1788–1866) ballad of Barbarossa the Emperor sends out his page, a dwarf, to look for the knowledgeable old ravens who will give a sign when the time has come.

Grimm's fairy tale (no. 181) 'The nixie of the millpond' is also a tale of reincarnation and points in its own way to processes we have already touched on from another angle. Following the advice of the old woman who has knowledge of destiny the young wife has liberated her husband, the huntsman, from the clutches of the nixie of the millpond. But hardly has he escaped from the element of water when the nixie tries to use the whole force of the pond to pull the fleeing couple into the depths where, in the ether life of the water, they will forget their egos.

If you have ever lain still in really warm water you will have experienced how the senses recede and you feel more and more encradled and rocked in a state of dream, until suddenly, at the last moment, being overcome by fear of not being able to return from it, you sit up with a jolt.

In this kind of fear the young wife calls to the wise old woman for help, and she transforms her into a toad and him into a frog. 'The flood that had overtaken them could not destroy them, but it tore them apart and carried them far away.'

In fairy tales water is often an image of the ether world, and also of life after death. Awaking from sleep we now and again experience something of this sphere. As though coming from another shore we are swimming over the sea or a wide river, or sailing in a boat. It is as though when we are in the element of water we are in the ether weaving of the other world.

But why does the old woman change the young wife into a toad and the huntsman into a frog? Toads and frogs belong, of course, zoologically to amphibians, in fact to the tailless ones that make a sound and can as it were stand up. The name amphibian (*amphi* = on both sides, *bios* = life) tells us as well that they can live both in water and on land, just as human beings can alternate between living on earth and in heaven without losing their identity. On the other hand the nixie wanted to keep their human part for herself in the element of water, thus cancelling out their identity and preventing reincarnation. Toads and frogs are also pictures indicating the ability of human beings to be at home in both worlds, and who are predestined to express their individual ego nature alternately in both realms.

The fairy tale continues. When the water had dispersed and they both touched dry land again they regained their human form, but neither knew where the other was; they found themselves among strange people who did not know their native land. High mountains and deep valleys lay between them. In order to keep themselves alive they were both obliged to tend sheep. For many long years they drove their flocks through field and forest and were full of sorrow and longing.

When spring had once more broken forth on the earth they both went out one day with their flocks, and as chance would have it they drew near each other. They met in a valley but did not recognize each other; yet they rejoiced that they were no longer so lonely. Henceforth they each day drove their flocks to the same place; they did not speak much but they felt comforted. One evening, when the full moon was shining in the sky, and the sheep were already at rest, the shepherd pulled the flute out of his pocket and played on it a beautiful but sorrowful air. When he had finished he saw that the shepherdess was weeping bitterly. 'Why are you weeping?' he asked. 'Alas,' answered she, 'thus shone the full moon when I played this tune on my flute for the last time, and the head of my beloved rose out of the water.' He looked at her, and it seemed as if a veil fell from his eyes, and he recognized his dear wife; and when she looked at him and the moon shone on his face she knew him also. They embraced and kissed each other, and no one need ask if they were happy.

Thus the two of them are reincarnated, and the longing for one another coming from subconscious wisdom brings them together through powerful forces of destiny. The sound of the flute awakens the memory of the past earth life where they lived and suffered together, and they recognize each other once more. Nothing is lost, yet are we capable of raising the treasure from the past so as to gain knowledge of it? We have to learn to recognize destiny and accept it gratefully.

Not to be born again was once considered the worst of fates. In the Song of Sigurd, Hagen curses Bruenhilde in the following words: 'May your sinister fate be fulfilled! Let no one interfere with your long path, and may you be prevented for ever from being born again.'[65]

Hagen's curse absolutely presupposes the concept of repeated earth lives.

A fairy tale from South West Africa tells of how the concept of reincarnation was lost again. The Hottentots tell the story of the moon giving the hare, as the cleverest animal,[66] the task of telling human beings that just as he, the moon, rises and sets and always returns again, they too, when they have completed one life on earth, will return again and again to the earth.[67] The hare promised to do this, but what he told human beings was that, just as he the hare did, they would only live once on earth. Although the moon was very angry that the hare had told human beings something so wrong, yet it was too late to do anything about it.

This hare-cleverness became the intellect that is directed towards the earth and which conceals heavenly wisdom from human beings. Because heavenly wisdom was concealed it has become apocryphal, occult and secret.[68]

Inborn Capacities

Talents and abilities

When applying for a job as a teacher or any other profession we are, on the one hand, asked about our skills and abilities, our qualifications, or about our aptitudes which could, given the right circumstances, be further developed. Or we are asked on the other hand about the experience we have already had, the skills we have already put into practice. In fact we can already see in children the abilities their destiny has provided them with, what they have brought with them into earth life. Experience and skills, however, are acquired only in the course of a lifetime. It is in the next earth life that these will show themselves as inborn abilities and skills.

Now what role does heredity — the bodily factor — play in giving physical effect to these inborn talents? For after all, the acquisition of abilities also requires certain bodily conditions.

A good musician strives to get a good instrument with which to further his art. One can hear from the playing of it whether the wrong notes are because the instrument is out of tune or because the player is incompetent. On the basis of the biographical reports we have already had (see pp. 122–33) we realize that musicality is brought into earth life as a natural gift, and therefore the person chooses parents who can put a suitable heritage at his/her disposal. That would be the hereditary factor.

A family of musicians, in which a person is choosing to incarnate if possible, will in addition to this be surrounded by friends of music and practising musicians — a circumstance which provides the stimulating environment which the individuality needs in order to become conscious of the intentions he brought with him.

Inherited qualities and environment have to be as close as possible to the intentions of the particular individuality who, for his part, has to bring along the talent.

Yet the most important prerequisite necessary for these intentions to be realized is the very will force of the individual to seek on the one hand for the right hereditary factors and on the other hand for the right milieu, so that his talent can actually come to expression.

Now and again, however, you notice people who are definitely gifted musically yet appear not to be interested in their talent. People such as this do their best to choose a profession for which they obviously have no gift, for which in fact they are absolutely unskilled. It is as though they wanted to acquire some new capacity for their next incarnation. Skills once acquired are not lost, for they can, as history shows us, appear again in the company of newly acquired ones (e.g. K.L. Schleich or Hans Carossa, who were both doctors and poets).

On the other hand it can also happen that although a person brings with him a good artistic gift paired with a strong-willed ego, he may — possibly because of thalidomide damage — not have grown any arms. He learns to paint with his feet, thus acquiring new capacities for his next life.

The question can now be asked as to how that kind of inborn gift arises altogether. Rudolf Steiner told us — and he gave examples he investigated occultly — that someone who for example had the opportunity to receive an abundance of musical impressions had nevertheless to let them pass him by unused as it were, because he did not have perfect pitch. But in the life between death and a new birth he felt the urge to become a practising musician in his next earth life.

Another person may have had a particularly strong connection to architectural forms, and experienced them as giving forth sound. The need then arises in him to produce the sounds himself. So he looks for a suitable set of parents for his next incarnation who can give him the possibility through the line of heredity (see p. 153) to create a suitable physical organ of hearing. And the environment, in the first instance his family, stimulate him psychologically to take up what his ego is looking for.

An inherited, good physical organization of hearing brings the most diverse individualities together in families, by way of which a common destiny for the future can be brought about. This explains for instance how it was that in the course of 250 years 29 musicians were born into the Bach family.

Mathematical gifts can occur in a family in as striking a manner as musical gifts do. The best known example of this, which Rudolf Steiner often described, is that of the Bernoulli family. Steiner refers to the fact[69] that for a mathematical gift no special brain construction is necessary, as many people believed. The thinking and logic of a mathematician was the same as other peoples. What it depends on is the instrument of the cochlea in the ear consisting of three bones positioned in the three directions of space. According to Benninghoff-Goerttler[70] these can show great individual fluctuations in form, length and curve. Rudolf Steiner stressed that it is the particular way these are formed which bring about a talent for mathematics. This supplies the physical aptitude for mathematics. It is a physical organ, and therefore has to be inherited accordingly. So we see eight significant mathematicians incarnating in the Bernoulli family.[71]

One has also to be talented to be a teacher, and many a person is pedagogically gifted to a high degree without having learnt it. The individuality happens to have brought the required ability along, though it sometimes requires several incarnations stretching over millennia in order to perfect the ability.

Thus an individuality can draw on capacities for which the foundations were laid thousands of years ago. A person often has several outstanding talents and cannot make up his mind which he would prefer to practise. Goethe, too, did not know at the age of 40 whether he had been born to be an artist or a poet.[72] So he not only painted pictures in poetic words but also taught anatomical drawing in Jena. We have already spoken about Adolf Portman (see pp. 127–8).

So we see that the basis is laid in a former life for talents, gifts and abilities which then often pass through metamorphoses. The ego, the spiritual core of the human being, is the actual carrier of these, and brings them along into earth life.

According to Rudolf Steiner, people who have acquired an abundance of knowledge in certain areas during one lifetime and have not only made good use of this knowledge but also been keen observers will, in the following incarnation, be 'given' an astral body with special gifts in those particular areas. Specially good examples of this are the journeymen of the Middle Ages who acquired 'proficiency' and much 'experience' on their travels. The experiences the ego acquires are in the next incarnation stamped into the astral body. On the other hand what people feel in the realm of joy and sorrow in their inner life works in the following incarnation right down into the ether body and brings about in them a lasting inclination for a particular thing, for instance a leaning to engage in music.

So in addition to the talents and the bodily organization these require, and which the individuality draws to himself through the hereditary stream, there is a third factor, the one that concerns the environment, and which is an area the ego also includes in its search for the right requirements. Parents, relatives and friends belong here.[73] The ego will endeavour to plan to meet with the right teachers, working relationships with colleagues, and many more such things, and also plan to find landscapes which will have a beneficial effect on the soul. The nationality and language is also a significant factor. The encounter with helpful fellow humans, also people who are harmful, is also often destined from the previous life (karma), though this is not always so. For we are continually creating new conditions of destiny for ourselves, especially in the second half of life. These can already have their effect in this earth life, but more especially they will carry a lot of weight in the early years of the next incarnation.

Thus in order to understand a person's destiny we have as it were to consider three factors: *the ego*, which brings with it a particular talent; *the soul*, which draws to it the right human relationships, and a suitable social milieu, receiving from it the stimulation it needs; and *the bodily basis*, i.e. the *physical body*, which follows by and large the laws of heredity, the *etheric body*, which shows an inclination towards an activity corresponding to an acquired talent, and the *astral body*, which contains experiences acquired in a previous life which encourage the soul to be open to the current situation in the environment.

So there is an overlapping, an interpenetrating of several factors in which we can discern a trichotomy of body, soul and spirit, just as the bodily vehicles also show a trinity of physical body, ether body and soul body (astral body). But the actual driving force is the ego.

Although we have had to forego giving any of Rudolf Steiner's accounts of actual individuals whom he has followed up in their succeeding incarnations, we have nevertheless referred to him time and again because he has given us the clearest, most detailed description of the way reincarnation and karma work with regard to talents and abilities. And the laws he has disclosed to us can be clearly understood by observing daily life. In fact many of life's events only become understandable when we include the point of view of reincarnation and karma, which develops in us a profound feeling for the truth of this view. This key for explaining the phenomena of life enables us to learn to understand life all the better. We become aware of a growing confidence in life.

Illness as destiny

At the conclusion of our considerations about human nature, where we have come as far as envisaging a prenatal life and repeated earth lives, let us now ask the question about illnesses, the disposition to illnesses and even the ultimate question of being born as a cripple. From the viewpoints we have reached of the laws of reincarnation is there an answer to the question as to the significance of being ill? How often do we ask ourselves 'Why am I being ill right now, and why is this illness hitting *me* in particular?' If we feel our way into these questions, approaching them as though trying to understand their inner purpose, we sometimes suspect that it had to be like this, that we needed it. How much have I learnt through going through the illness! We sense that illness can be a learning process.

But have we not already spoken about 'learning processes' of this kind? After all, this is the only way to cure psychosomatic illnesses. And is not the acquiring of talents and abilities also this kind of learning process for the ego, as we saw in the last chapter? We spoke about the experiences from the previous earth life being stamped onto the astral body. So we bring along as it were in our astral bodies characteristic qualities and ways of behaving stemming from a previous incarnation. A wise guidance of our destiny — and surely we can see Christ at work here — leads the course of our development between death and a new birth in such a way that we are given the opportunity in our following or subsequent earth lives to make up for omissions and onesidednesses.

Let an example given by Rudolf Steiner demonstrate the point. He describes how people fall prey to diphtheria in the next life if in the previous one their actions were prompted by 'all sorts of emotional outbursts and suchlike'.

What effect does a strong emotion have on our bodily vehicles? The blood is whipped into movement, one goes red in the face, the heart beats faster — and the person talks incessantly.

Diphtheria is an inflammatory illness which attacks the mucous membranes of the throat and sometimes of the nose too, but chiefly those of the larynx and, moving further down, the windpipes. It is the physical process corresponding to emotion on the soul level. In this severe state of illness a person can hardly speak, in fact there can be periods of breathlessness and general paralysis. The heart, too, can be affected.

It is the qualities and ways of behaviour stamped on the astral body from a former earth life which dispose a person in the first place to an illness, and this, and this alone, is what makes a person open to infection. This is one of the directions from which a person's bodily constitution is determined. Rudolf Steiner then says that not every disposition to illness is bound to lead to an illness. People can transform tendencies to illness if they practise self-knowledge and carry out inner activity regularly. If parents and teachers notice a certain character weakness appearing in a child they can lovingly help it to deal with it so that the weakness is balanced out and harmonized.

Sometimes, though, it is necessary to be strict rather than indulgent. The following accounts show how naturally children in situations of illness will turn to the idea of reincarnation.

There was an eight-year-old girl so seriously ill with leukaemia that her mother knew she would die soon. So the child comforted her mother by saying: 'For goodness sake don't be so miserable—of course I will come back!'

In another family a four-and-a-half-year-old girl was visiting her cousins. Eight months previously this girl's little two-and-a-half-year-old cousin had died, and both families had spoken a lot about the terrible misfortune. In the course of the afternoon the mother of the surviving two-year-old sister heard the visiting cousin say with great enthusiasm to the toddler: 'How big you have grown! When your brother comes down again he *will* be pleased to see how you have changed!'[74]

The most difficult health impediment is probably to be handicapped either physically or mentally. But against the background of what has gone before we may be able to feel our way towards the fact, or perhaps even understand, that even destinies of this kind are not meaningless. Everything signifies for the people hit by it and for the relatives a task through which they can grow. Our ego, our spiritual core, does not grow strong if all the stones are removed from its path, and all burdens taken away. On the contrary! The more there is to overcome, all the more energetic, healthier and stronger a person can be in their next life. It should also be said that we do not only bring along our own allotted destiny, for in the course of social existence there is always new destiny arising. Impediments can therefore also be something individuals have chosen to take upon them-selves. However, souls can only take up this kind of choice with the help of higher spiritual beings, even the Christ, and, out of insight into a higher necessity, be better able to serve the whole of humankind in the next life. And this will succeed all the better the more the people tending the handicapped person help to carry the affliction from out of the power of the Christ.

The following report is a fitting one to end with.

Katie, paralysed from birth, had been bedridden for 20 years. Now her limbs were withering, and the two doctors who were in charge of her in the home were expecting her to die.

They had arranged things in the home in such a way that Katie was surrounded by the other children and what they were doing, so that she could be a part of it although she could not sing along with them nor had she ever spoken a word — in fact she could not join in what they were doing at all. When in the hour before her death the doctors wanted to enter her room they heard singing ringing out through the closed door. When they opened it they saw Katie sitting up in bed for the first time, singing all the songs that had been sung around her. Then she lay down and died peacefully.

We can think of this person taking into the spiritual world, as a gift, all the experiences lovingly given her by the children, the nurses and the doctors. Nothing that is of the nature of the spirit world is ever lost. And we can picture Katie in her next earth life busily at work as a forceful personality active in a human community, for she will have brought with her a lifelong impulse to be socially active.

Concluding thoughts

In the stories and accounts we have given here it has been evident that not only can Rudolf Steiner, on the basis of his spiritual-scientific research, present and vouch for a life after death which leads right through to a new birth, but that also among many peoples a knowledge of these facts still exists or at least has been preserved in traditional myths and fairy tales.

If we think back to the dreams and visions announcing the arrival of children, then the idea of an existence before conception becomes a real perception.

The soul of the child makes itself known and tells us about the unique destiny it wants to bring to expression. As spiritual beings the individual people preparing to incarnate already bear within them their value and dignity as human beings, which they will then strive to bring to realization in the course of their earthly lives. To be in good hope is an expression, in German, which is synonymous with being pregnant. Why do they say 'to have good hope?' We really do feel hopeful with our whole hearts if something spiritual reaches down to us from heaven. We hope for, actually expect the genuine humanhood we are striving towards to come about in us through light and strength from above. That would be the deeper meaning of self-realization—that we can unfold in ourselves our human worth and dignity.

It is like this too for a mother who is expecting a child. A heavenly presence descends on her and, as we saw, many mothers experience it like this. It is as though a child—the spiritual core of a human being who is incarnating—brings heavenly light along with it. And mothers often feel that they are inwardly strengthened and can defy every difficulty. You can recognize a young mother by the way she becomes beautiful. And what has shone forth from the mother's face still dreams on as an angelic presence from the eyes of babies. Through its radiant being a small child brings a heavenly message down onto the earth, and this can give us hope for the future of mankind. The deeper, inner meaning of all the experiences described only becomes clear to us when we compare one account with another and begin to see a regular pattern in the course of events. The statements mutually support one another and comparing them shows us the truth in them and how they can be interpreted.

This is how we get an answer to the question about the actual nature of a human being we are receiving and have to bring to birth. The eternal spiritual core of the child already exists before conception and will continue to exist after death.

The idea of reincarnation is not in opposition to Christianity but only to Church dogma. Nor does it contradict scientifically found facts, but it does contradict their materialistic interpretation. Against the background of reincarnation we can, with the help of art, science and religion, create a picture of the human being in its wholeness which includes, besides the bodily nature, the real nature of both soul and spirit. This view also throws a completely new light on the problem of overpopulation. In the course of humanity's evolution there have always been times when there have been more people living on the earth. Some individuals spend shorter periods between death and rebirth, other people longer ones. Rudolf Steiner once said that in the twentieth century all the existing individuals would incarnate at least once, which was also connected with the speed-up of the tempo of evolution. And after this the spaces between incarnations will get longer again. We can assume that this alone would bring about a reduction in the size of the population on earth.

Those advanced calculations regarding population can also be compared to saying that a young person between the second and the fifteenth year is becoming on average 6 cm taller per year, so that at 50 years of age people would be 3 m and at the age of 90 5.4 m tall. This is presupposing that the increase in height would continue right up to people's death. But because we know that an increase in height goes in bursts—in the ninth year a child actually puts on an extra 7.5 cm[75]—and is more or less finished by the age of 20, and because we also know that nobody grows to a height of either 3 m or 5.4 m, we no longer depend on calculations. And also, with regard to the population figure, more and more new individuals would, theoretically, have to be created, ad infinitum, if the world population were to continue to grow at this rate after the year 2000. In fact the rate of population increase is already declining, even among nations that use neither the pill nor any other method of contraception. Moreover, individualities who had never incarnated before would bring with them no capacities for which the basis would have to have been laid in previous incarnations and won through grappling with earth experiences, as we have seen. They would also bring no destined relationships, no karma with them. They would be the sort of people who would not fit into our world at all. But we do not know of anything like that. There are obviously still some individuals who appear to have had only a few incarnations on earth, as for example the so-called Stone Age men living in the remote jungles of Mindanao (one of the Philippine Islands), who were not discovered until 1971, and who have no idea what the concepts 'enemy' and 'war' mean. Like the Unambal in north-western Australia they are in course of dying out. An individual leaves the body of this Negrito at death and looks out a new body for itself in the next incarnation where it will meet with different life situations and be able to develop further on a soul-spiritual level.

In referring to what is called a population problem, which in fact is no such thing, we are brought—on the foundation of what we have been presenting—above all face to face with the question: when we perform an abortion, what are we doing to these children's souls, to these individualities who want to incarnate and are striving to develop further? We see that from this point of view we carry our share of responsibility for the whole evolution of humankind. In a similar way the whole question of freedom, which is usually confused with arbitrary choice, presents itself quite differently. All human relationships, social questions and political decisions will have to change when looked at from the point of view of the life before birth, existence before conception.

HARTMUT GOERG

The Will to Live a New Life

The Meaning of Biography and the Rhythms of Life

To learn to see the rhythms in one's own life and to experience them consciously can be a great help to every one of us. Being aware of them leads more and more to it becoming second nature for us to have a feeling for the larger rhythms of our existence and the meaning of our life on earth. Our life between birth and death is gradually recognized to be only a section of our total existence which takes place in a cosmic context in the rhythm of constantly repeating earth lives which are new each time.

Whilst living on earth we 'breathe' our life in and 'breathe' it out again in the time spent between death and a new life. In the course of our life we 'breathe' our earthly consciousness in every day and 'breathe' it out again at night. The rhythm we know best — the *smallest rhythm* — is breathing air in and out. The *largest breathing rhythm* of our lives is something we have to get to know again as a process that repeats.

In a *Platonic year* of 25,920 years[1] a human life of about 72 years is contained 360 times. A year has approximately 360 days. A person's life contains accordingly about 25,920 days, and each day we breathe in and out about 25,920 times. Hidden within this play of numbers is deep cosmic wisdom out of which arises the many rhythms in our life.

We would be justified in presuming that in a subtle way laws of this kind exist throughout life and could throw light on the whole of our higher existence. In the phases of rhythmic change taking place in the course of human life, along with the experiences of destiny that occur, it is possible for us to experience the reality of pre-existence, life after death and thoughts on reincarnation.

Remaining with the image of the breathing rhythms of world existence, we begin to breathe a new life in the pre-birth phase. Or we awaken again to a new 'earth day' out of sleep in the spiritual world. A proper 'awakening' out of this sleeping phase to independent earthly consciousness only begins at puberty, when human beings begin to see their earthly existence as a confrontation between the world and their own ego. Looking at it this way we can regard our childhood as a period in which all the spiritual beings and all the human beings in our life are surrounding and protecting us, preparing us for an independent earth life. This period seems like a dream prior to awakening.

Striking phases of change take place at the transition from one seven-year period to another. Our lives are marked by ten such nodal points. Each seven-year transition gives a person the opportunity to take a big step forward in their development. In the first third of life, up till 21, these transformations are externally visible (change of teeth, puberty, coming of age). From 28 onwards the changes are chiefly steps in inner maturity. Only at the age of 49 does our outer appearance appear to predominate again, and this phase is marked by disagreeable signs of ageing. However, it is correct to say that in the 'years of change' the most significant transformation is in the direction of spiritual maturity — an inner process that calls for a corresponding outer loss, yet this can have rewarding consequences.

I am going to give a short characterization of the course of life in order to stimulate self-knowledge, knowledge of the spirit, and an understanding of life before conception. I would like to take the span from puberty to death (the conscious earth phase), omit the body-free period between death and conception and end with childhood. May this unusual order of the human course of life from youth to childhood contribute to loosening up a lot of the rigid boundaries of our existence between birth and death. Perhaps some of you will receive, at the close of childhood, a powerful flash of memory of the 'body-free' period (which I cannot elucidate with examples), and be helped to a profound understanding of the desire on the part of unborn souls to live a new life on earth.

As young people awaken to a conscious understanding of the world and of themselves as a part of a whole, they are thus exercising their thinking until by the time they are 21 they can use it independently. Their bodily nature assumes the expression of spiritual, individual maturity, as it reaches adult proportions. The ego is born visibly in the world.

Bodily maturity reaches its first completion. *Soul maturity* takes its course from age 21 to 42, and *spiritual maturity*, covering the last third of life, brings earth's pilgrimage to a close with the phase that concludes with death.

After puberty the ego still lives in an unfree state in a life of soul that is strongly polarized. A boy's experience covers a wide field between the world of the senses and the inner world; with girls it is more inward. Young persons have a growing need to engage with other people out of forces of sympathy and antipathy, sometimes developing crushes on people older than themselves, or overestimating themselves and consequently condemning other people. With their peers they form groups in which they exchange ideas and try out newly discovered ones.

The etheric body, which has now become free (see pp. 53–5), brings out of pre-existence unconscious memories which now encounter intimations of the future. This leads to imaginative abilities, which develop into a leaning towards a higher kind of love (eros), into an artistic sensitivity which leads to aesthetics. A desire for active engagement with the world outside stirs the realm of the will and eventually presses towards acquiring judgements.

Treichler describes this age in the following way. In the last resort the person is using his own judgement in his search for the nature of the object, the essence of the world, the core of existence out of which it arises and out of which it can arise again in thinking (which one has achieved oneself).[2]

What is finally arrived at in the coming together of the female and male principle out of healthy soul forces and a conscious recognition of the ego is the will to take responsibility for a future human being. To quote Treichler: 'The creative forces of the etheric body, which were active in the person's own body up to the seventh year, can now become creative in the begetting of another body.'

With the 'birth of the ego' at 21 independence of the individuality and questions about one's own existence grow stronger. We go in search of finding our own self mirrored in the life of the cosmos and discovering an understanding of our own individual relationship to the world and to humankind.

This step is accompanied by a maturing of the soul in the direction of acquiring a more conscious grasp of the higher dimension of our existence, our spiritual origin, and to bring it to an unfolding within ourselves.

If we regard the first three seven-year periods as the phase of awakening to individual earthly consciousness in the process of taking hold of our earthly body to the point of independence, this is based on a constant force of *will* which goes through a transformation from one seven-year period to the next. To start with the will is of a perceptive nature, working on the forming of the body in conjunction with the sense organs (nourishment and building up of one's own body from out of the environment), then it changes around the age of seven into a kind of will that is of a feeling nature, by means of which the child experiences its own inner soul life in pictures (nourishment and building up of the life of soul from out of archetypal pictures). And at 14 the phase begins when the will is of a cognitive nature (the nourishing and building up of the spiritual 'I' from out of the world of concepts), the schooling of thought.

Then the middle third of life (21–42) can be looked on as the phase of acquiring independence in *feeling* with regard to our connection to the whole context of existence. It is now the turn of feeling to go through tranformation from perceiving the world, through a thorough inwardizing of our feeling towards existence by way of a process of deepening our soul forces, and the increasing wakefulness of our forces of understanding as far as the level of the 'consciousness soul'. During this period of the soul's maturing there is already the dawning of a spiritual consciousness, *knowing born of feeling*.

In the last third of life (42–63) a person is capable of achieving these metamorphoses in *thinking*. A perceptual perceiving of the way things are connected (our life's aims become clearer) is followed by a conceptual inwardizing, sensing (stopping to consider carefully), and finally by the ability to recognize the essence of things in conceptual form, which is the highest achievement we can attain in earth life.

All of the three large sections of life, when looked at together, show a transition, from perceiving (will) to soul experience (feeling) to spiritual knowing (thinking).

Problems concerned with destiny can be better understood and accepted after the midpoint of life. Illnesses can also be more easily accepted and the possibilities that they bring for further development can be acknowledged. Whether in one's own case or that of other people for whom one is caring — to be aware of the deeper significance of these everyday phenomena will contribute to spiritual maturing.

At this central point of our life development we can have

a clear inkling of the whole span of our existence covering repeated earth lives. Bodily development does not culminate until 35, after which an increased death process contributes to serving the build-up of spiritual growth.

Visualizing this rhythmic inhalation and exhalation of life on earth and knowing about what happens after death can also be of great help to the dying.

Discussion about a 'dignified, meaningful death' can happen only if the approach of death is accepted as a natural event and there is an inkling of what is to follow death. If a person is having these near-death experiences then many spiritual threads connected with the after-life may possibly lend themselves to be discussed. This helps with letting go of earthly ties. The perception of the shining in of spiritual light coming through the gate of death, which happens in the last phase of life, can be comforting and releasing.

Anyone who can accompany a dying person in this way can gain strength for his own life's aims and is filled with fresh anticipatory hope for the period prior to a new birth. If death and birth are once more felt to be natural transitional phases in the span of our existence then confidence can also arise in an existence after death and prior to a new birth. The circle of our life is completed if we then envisage childhood as a preparation for the *conscious* part of our earthly existence. Step by step a small child masters the world of space as it learns to walk, speak and think. After the change of teeth, which expresses a discarding of the last of the 'inherited' body, the development of a strong soul life can begin. Childhood diseases can be seen as important impulses exercised each time by the child's ego to bring about important steps in development. As the second seven-year period draws to a close the child's organism now awakens to a thinking consciousness — to earthly maturity.

Questions Concerning Conception

Parents who want children but do not have them despite being fertile

I often meet with couples who have been trying unsuccessfully for years to have a child. Many doctors had already tried giving them hormone treatment and partly, too, artificial insemination, despite there being no definite evidence of either anatomical or hormonal defects. They remained childless.

In course of conversation it frequently transpired that they had a strongly demanding attitude to having a child. They were thinking in a materialistically logical sense that just as with any other natural creation or even a technical apparatus one could be produced on demand. To acquire the 'product' it should be sufficient to express the wish to have one. Consequently a great many people let themselves be drawn into the mechanization of child 'production' through the use of hormones and exact timing. Many children are even produced this way.

If we succeed in picking out the reality of the individual from out of the whole span of human existence and can go as far as accepting its existence before conception, then we soon recognize in the unborn being an individual will. It brings a great feeling of relief to the partners no longer to feel forced to have sexual intercourse in accordance with the timing of the end of ovulation but when they both feel drawn to it. Even finishing with hormone therapy can be felt to be a relief. Married life becomes harmonious again!

Knowing that the willed intention of an individuality wanting to incarnate disregards the timing of its mother's ovulation and can frequently alter it to suit its own cosmic constellation can work to overcome compulsory restrictions. In fact many children are conceived at a totally unexpected time (see p. 178).

Most of these 'healthy' couples, when they let go completely of the thought of a child and their often tense desire to have one, have 'their' child very soon without any help at all from a third party—by giving up work for instance.

The well-known phenomenon that when a couple adopt a child this is often followed by a child of their own confirms allowing the child its freedom to exercise its own will to incarnate. Compulsion puts many children off.

In one case I was told that through a conscious effort to overcome an egoistic desire to have a child—and also without adoption—a child eventually came who later on was always very self-willed.

If in the phase after the thirty-fifth year childless couples still have an egoistically inclined desire to have a child they can easily suffer from a feeling of panic that the door has closed (the general opinion nowadays goes to encourage this). In fact this phenomenon often appears from 30 onwards. An understanding of the spiritual aspect not only cures one of egoism but also rids one of worrying about not being able to have a child any longer.

However, in place of this the problem also arises to *want to have one's own child* with the help of all the external aids possible today, although the means of achieving this by way of one's own body appears closed. Justified doubts must arise, when nowadays parent's egoism permits the conceiving of a child by artificial insemination. Is this method not a travesty of the wise design of a socially human order, especially in view of the countless abortions by means of which a meaningful entry into a human life is broken off? People who think further constantly see the contradiction even without the help of anthroposophy.

One can also think further about the idea of gene

manipulation by means of which unfavourable inherited tendencies can be exchanged for 'normal' ones. In this process the child chosen by the parents follows automatically — which is surely the opposite of individually willed intentions for a person's new life on earth, in which a soul may even 'want' the destiny of having a handicap.

Parents with fertility disorders

On the whole what has just been said applies also to people with fertility disorders, if we can take our departure from the fact that a child is capable of removing or avoiding hindrances in the parents so that it can succeed in living its *own* life with these parents.

There are many reports giving evidence of the fact that in cases of fertility disorders caused by either anatomical or functional defects pregnancies have nevertheless occurred. We have heard of children arriving in cases of 'confirmed' sterility, i.e. where a blockage of the oviduct has been confirmed both before and after pregnancy.

One of the first couples in England who, because of evident anatomical sterility, had a child by artificial insemination had a further child soon afterwards born under completely natural conditions.

At the beginning of my activity as a gynaecologist both my colleagues and myself were not a little surprised when a patient who had had both oviducts removed (due each time to pregnancies occurring in the oviduct) appeared with a normal pregnancy and had three further children after this one. In technical literature there is a report from the USA of a case of a living child being born by Caesarean section which, due to a missing uterus (through an operation) had almost reached full term in the abdominal cavity.

The frequent almost daily slip-ups with reliable contraceptives, a fact that defies definite clarification, also shows the ability children have of succeeding in coming.

In some cases of patients who lack the signs of normal functioning of their abdominal organs (no ovulation or no period over many years) I have witnessed pregnancies occurring, without any hormone treatment. A particular couple had a child despite the fact that there was proof of the husband's sterility (very few sperms and no success with hormone therapy). This was after we had had a conversation during which both partners had fully given up the idea of a child of their own.

Nevertheless a natural feeling can arise in parents that they ought to accept help either in the anatomical direction (operation to repair an organ) or in the functional direction (hormone treatment) to smooth the way for the child's sake. This could be regarded as a responsible action on the parent's part because it is wanted by the child.

Parents who are sterile

If there are no further possibilities of bringing about a pregnancy from the bodily point of view (no germ cells), then as a rule a normal pregnancy is impossible. A pregnancy brought about artificially by means of foreign germ cells is no doubt far removed from a social relationship between parents and child that arises naturally. In cases such as this egoistic interests drive out a willingness to be able to accept, unselfishly, an adopted child.

If there is, however, among parents in this situation the unselfishness and the readiness to take on responsibility, then they usually solve their problem by adopting. Looking at existence as a whole the situation of sterile couples can be understood much better if considered as a matter of destiny. In understanding the situation and individually coming to terms with it people can experience further developments of another kind in their lives which are beneficial and that were previously undreamt of.

Adoption

The wish to have a child is often exaggerated, and when it is unfulfilled it is difficult to separate from one's own body. If the misgivings regarding an unknown line of heredity can finally be overcome this is often a release, too, from one's own egoity. A selfless attitude to an adopted child has now been arrived at.

In addition, obtaining an adoption is difficult and troublesome. To acquire a child is a real fight. Going through it, however, means that the feeling of responsibility for the little person is increased tremendously. As the advice to mothers to have an abortion exceeds to such an extent the number of mothers who have surviving unwanted children, only a few parents willing to adopt can get one.

When I hear conversations about caring for unwanted children I repeatedly hear the statement: 'If I do have a child then at least I want to bring it up myself!' On the other hand one often hears the argument: 'I wouldn't bring a child into such a bad world as this!' When, however, they hear of the reality of there being a fully valid human existence even before birth, of reincarnation and of the child's indomitable will to live its own life on earth, there are still many women prepared to let their child come. They are also not inclined to give their child up for adoption. In one case only was there an obvious readiness to do so. Yet the mother became so strongly involved with the child during pregnancy that she was also able to keep it. And she became a very happy mother.

An experience of destiny shows us clearly how much wisdom is contained in social relationships. The path of an Indian child who, at the age of four months, more 'by chance' than anything else, went to a German family is characterized by profound inner connecting links with her adoptive parents. To this day (the child is now eight years of age) the parents have never doubted that this individuality is their child. Through the idea of reincarnation they cannot avoid the impression that it is a case of a person needing a non-European body to be able to build special faculties in life by means of being in Middle Europe, and in this particular family with its broad social setting. There may nowadays be roundabout ways from the Third World to us through adoption, if contraceptives bar the way, yet a suitable social environment is nevertheless being sought. Rudolf Steiner specifies that in future, social connections arising between people will play a far more decisive role than heredity.[3] Parent-child relationships will then become independent of whoever brought the child into the world.

I told a lot of my patients this story, and it not only encouraged many adoptions but, later on, I was also given reports confirming 'miraculous' inner relationships with these children.

Planning conception with a knowledge of pre-existence

There are various well-known possibilities for preventing conception. After a rational consideration of the pros and cons an individual chooses the one most suitable for her. If, however, the patient is open to spiritual considerations the discussion can include a further method. More people are prepared for this than one might expect today. Extending the matter of prevention to the supersensible realm presents a totally new possibility. The idea of reincarnation, pre-existence and existence after death can be fully included. With this method the child is as it were brought into the whole picture. It is in the parents' consciousness all the time. Which other method considers the child at all? The very idea of preventing conception excludes the child.

How can an actual awareness of the unborn child come about? Anyone with the experience of what can be perceived by the heart can also have an inkling of how we access spiritual/soul sources. This kind of sensitivity is certainly present in many people today — they just do not want to admit to the reality behind it. 'Observations of that kind could make me embarrassingly conspicuous or see me regarded as crazy' is the way some of them respond consciously to these emotions. Others are afraid of them and do not dare talk about them.

Rudolf Steiner's spiritual science can be of positive help here. With his detailed descriptions of life before conception and after death he confirms all these intimations. To people going through a training in this area and who school and refine their thinking ability, these higher mysteries become pictures. They begin to see themselves connected with the pictured being until its characteristics are so clearly seen that an inner exchange takes place. The idea of repeated earth lives and the reality of human existence before conception then becomes self-evident. The willed intention of a human being to take its way from the spiritual world into a new life on earth is then clearly seen. A person with this knowledge discovers that there is a being lovingly longing for parents and who is in search of its path to its new life on earth. Rudolf Steiner tells us that this path begins with seeing a process of ancestors, until finally the right couple appears at the end of the row. Every situation of the incoming being's destiny, the causes of which lie in the time before conception, are planned in advance and taken up into the will, although these are forgotten in our externalized, earthly consciousness. So the coming of a child to its parents is a re-encounter which they planned to happen. If we now include Rudolf Steiner's findings about matters of contraception we arrive at totally new concepts: preventing a human being from coming to earth; preventing destiny from happening; putting an obstacle in the way of the wise guidance of human existence and of human relationships! If we are in a position to perceive the being of an unborn child we shall always be faced with the question: Do we want to place ourselves at the service of guiding powers, and look at precautionary methods against the background of the highest considerations regarding human kind and cosmic existence, or not?

In this respect each human being today, through the very fact of our having in the natural course of evolution acquired individual freedom, has to make his or her very own decision on asking the question: 'Do I put my trust in the wisdom of higher beings of a divine order and take on the responsibility for the child who is entering earthly life, for my own sake and for the sake of these aims, or do I hinder the child wanting to come to me and share a common destiny?' Rational goals of an external nature (one's work, not wanting to keep house or to be tied to a child) often take pride of place.

If the patient I am talking to about these matters seems open to these intimations it is sufficient to point out the possibility of including having the experience of the coming child. The ability to do this is described by Rudolf Steiner as one that will be a normal capacity of humankind in the future. If the patient shows a willingness she will choose the way of a clear and conscious relationship to the unborn child. To help her over her hesitancy in these matters she can complement them by also practising the symptothermal method,[4] and during a fertile phase be open to whether a child is wanting to come.

Regarding this method let us remember an example from the first chapter of this book. It is about a mother of two children who, after the second child, decided to apply the above method. On receiving a vivid message it was an obvious matter to decide to have the child. Now, years later, she knows how right this decision was!

Two further examples:

After the birth of her third child a 26-year-old mother came to me very determined that she would now have to do something to make absolutely sure she would have no more children. She could neither take the responsibility for any more nor find the strength to cope with them. Surely the best thing to do was to go for a clear-cut solution, namely, sterilization. The pill and the coil she ruled right out. She felt quite clearly that another child would otherwise soon choose to come. The ensuing conversation included in detail all the problems that beset an individual. The fact that she was still so young presented sterilization in a very problematic light.

After our conversation the patient decided to apply the symptothermal method. In course of time, however, her assiduousness weakened, and she let another child come. She knew immediately, at the moment of conception, that a child was involved. Five weeks later she came to me to have her pregnancy confirmed. Although, to start with, she had doubted whether she was capable of accepting the child, she felt in the meantime, in the face of every reasonable argument, that this child belonged to her. All feelings of coercion had evaporated in both her and her husband — in fact they felt so much freer. Her husband is known to have said: 'Now we are *really* complete!'

Let me add a further remark. Often in the course of discussing preventive methods the natural methods were discarded in an uncritical way because the menstrual cycle was too irregular and therefore presented too much uncertainty. The very fact of a regular cycle, however, can induce carelessness in keeping the criteria in mind, which is evident from the above example. Ovulation, which is dependent on the cosmos, particularly the moon, does not have to coincide with the more important conception deadline of the child. If the child, as individual, requires a different day for conception from the one picked by the mother, ovulation is shifted to the right day. How obvious these arrangements can seem to many a woman who looks back on them long after the children have been born can be seen from the following example.

A 36-year-old patient was looking for a method of contraception suitable for her situation, the question of an abortion having already been raised when she was expecting her third unwanted child. Up till then the only contraceptive she had used was that in which the basal temperature is taken, yet all her pregnancies, according to the temperature curves, had always started soon after the period and not at the expected maternal ovulation (method according to Knaus-Ogino). She was always prepared to affirm the life of her children. The positive effect that was brought about by the third child in the family considerably changed the patient's relationship to her use of a contraceptive, which had been previously more routine. She began to be aware of the subtle qualities in the children and the important tasks in their destiny. Looking back at the pregnancy, she could remember each time a clear inner encounter with the child preceding conception. She could no longer bear to have to eliminate these inner connections through the external use of contraceptive methods. After our conversation she decided, with relief, to use the symptothermal method and to be more vigilant.

Several examples from the first part of this book show

that it is possible to refuse individually to accept a child whose presence one has been aware of. It can happen, though, that a child in this situation will go on 'pulling' and 'pushing' its parents to try and make them have it after all.

Sterilization

Without any health grounds

It happens not infrequently that after a couple have had all the children they want they decide to find a final solution to the matter of 'family planning'. They often consider sterilization. In these situations the decision is often made out of panic, without their being able to look beyond the present circumstances. But anyone who, after being sterilized, feels a child pushing to come into a new earth life will clearly feel something like the pain of deprivation. Yet there can be no fulfilment any more either for the wishful longing of the child to have its life or for the wish it arouses in the mother to have the child.

This aspect shows very clearly that a preventive measure of this kind puts a final barrier in the way of any wise ordering of karma. Women who regret having taken this step are often met with today attending a gynaecologist's surgery. The following are two contrasting examples.

A 26-year-old patient comes to my surgery one day, about a year after the birth of her third child, in floods of tears, demanding that I should send her immediately to a clinic to be sterilized. She could not cope with contraception any other way, and on no condition did she want more children. I could see that the patient was in a state of panic and was not at the moment capable of deciding for herself. In that state it was not possible for her to be able to size up future situations. For this reason I did not think it advisable to send her to be sterilized.

In the case of a 45-year-old patient who came to me wanting to be sterilized a short conversation sufficed for her to realize that it would be inadvisable to have the operation. Being calm and openminded she could easily see that she bore a responsibility towards the unlikely possibility of becoming pregnant at this stage. She wanted to stay with the natural contraceptive method she had been using, and if higher powers were to send her a child she would accept it. This last example is very typical of the level of maturity of a patient of this age. Similarly, a 30-year-old is considerably more likely to want to be sterilized than someone over 40, assuming of course that it is coupled with a clarifying conversation covering the whole picture.

In cases of illness

If an illness on the part of the parents could result in the child acquiring a hereditary illness (this does not mean a disability!), or a pregnancy and birth could threaten the mother's life, then sterilization obviously assumes quite another aspect. Actual doubts regarding the decision to sterilize are then hardly likely to occur.

If one of the partners shows symptoms of an illness the possibility is still there for them to come to a responsible decision on a spiritual/soul level, if they are aware of pre-existence. A renouncing of intercourse altogether would be a huge sacrifice – an unusual practice in the light of present-day opinion – although this would be rising to the highest level of human dignity. If this decision were freely undertaken, however, this abstemious act would show strong will-power and magnanimity.

Pregnancy

The supersensible aspects of an incarnation

The longing to be able to add a kind of balance to past lives arouses in an individual's spirit/soul being whilst in the pre-birth realm the tremendous urge to enter a new life. The highest hierarchies of angels help the reawakened ego being to prepare an earthly form to suit the person's individuality. What a wonderful way this wisdom-filled prototype of the human form comes to expression in earthly life compared to the poverty-stricken earthly form thought up in the 'scientific' theories of materialistic thinking and which is expected to conform to statistics or random change! How lacking in spirit and soul, how merely technical and mechanical would a person be if programmed entirely on the basis of chromosomes, genes and protein molecules! Only a stereotype robot can result from the kind of 'life-shaping' information supplied by the sort of 'knowledge' residing in the world of matter. Nothing that makes a person individual, nothing arising as a unique creation from pre-existence, could fit into this mass-produced copy of a human being. At this point we should already mention the question of the possibility of gene manipulation and artificial insemination (pp. 220–1). The human body is formed on the principles prepared by the highest divine beings. To become aware of these forces and to endeavour to welcome these souls returning to earth with the same kind of loving feelings that they themselves have is of the greatest service to the future of humankind. The awakening of their ego being in readiness for a new life is accompanied by trust in and love for their parents — a love that can be likened to that which streams towards us as the light of Christ in the hour of our death.

In the sort of 'family planning' common today this kind of action springing from love is becoming rarer and rarer. A self-centred intention on the part of the parents cannot be the sole basis for a new human life. The motive for parenthood could possibly be a highly developed, selfless feeling of responsibility for the individual will of the child which will need educational guidance until it is grown up. The child's life intentions need, for the fulfilling of its destiny, suitable parents (both the right individualities and the right stream of heredity) with the right kind of maturity, or immaturity, the right social environment and the right place of birth, with exactly the right cosmically meaningful timings. The moment of conception and of birth are of great importance. With regard to this Rudolf Steiner says that the cosmic moment is stamped onto the brain and has its effect on everything that follows.[5]

As well as the right moment of birth the individuality, in readiness for its new earthly path, also has to seek out the right hereditary influences, both of a favourable and an unfavourable kind (illnesses, disabilities, abilities, etc.) that will be needed for its individual destiny. In addition, the place where it will live is important from the point of view of how it will be affected in its chosen path of destiny. This can bring us to wonder at the diversity of the individual factors possible for one human life! If the inner relationship that the human being has to its parents before it has been conceived is very close (common paths of destiny) then the ability to perceive these relationships by the parents and the people closely involved with the child is becoming easier and easier these days. In the periodical *Eltern* (Parents) of March 1985, Prof. Peter Petersen describes clairvoyant capacities of parental couples in connection with conception. Regarding this theme Rudolf Steiner says the following:

> The individual who is incarnating brings the loving couple together. The archetypal being that is intent on incarnating has, as we said, become attached to its astral substance, and this astral substance now affects the passionate feelings of love. The movement occurring in the astral passion on earth mirrors the astral being of the descending individual... And if we think this thought through we have to say that the reincarnating human being is definitely involved in the choice of its parents. We see that in a certain sense the child loves its parents beforehand, even before impregnation, and is therefore drawn to them. Parental love is therefore the response to the child's love, it is reciprocal love.

In the first part of this book there is confirmation of people's increasing clairvoyant capacity.

In connection with the entering in of a new human being Rudolf Steiner says that in Eastern people an ability will develop to recognize the individual desiring to incarnate (eugenic occultism).

An awareness of conception and the first presentiment of the arrival of a child

The more I involve myself with this phenomenon, all the more, as a gynaecologist, do I become convinced that a pregnancy should be considered as beginning not with conception but with the first awareness of a child. Conception occurs somewhere along the course of this metaphysical/physical 'pregnancy'. The actual working out of dates is irrelevant. It is solely the individuality involved that determines the length of this 'pregnancy'.

A feeling of this kind generates awe and respect for the process and an increasing wariness of one-sided decisions to obstruct a path of incarnation (prevention, abortion, inducement). The accepting of a child becomes more a matter of course.

If a woman is aware of a child early on, and she feels the time until conception occurs to be a time for feeling 'expectant' in the same way as one does when pregnant then, in this same sense, a loving, trusting, joyful relationship will come about between the mother and the child.

Example:
A patient of mine had just reached a very satisfactory situation in her professional life and was keen on following it up and reaping the benefits. She was taking precautions by using the symptothermal method consciously, but to be quite safe she had a coil fitted.

In this satisfying situation she was all the more surprised when her husband told her, and this was a most unusual thing to come from him, that he had become aware of a child. He himself could hardly understand why he felt so strongly about this wish for a child. In the first conversation I had with her about this—while she was desperately resisting it—I took her again through all the aspects of pre-existence and karmic connections which were well known to her theoretically. We agreed to allow a week for reflection. After only a few days the certainty had arisen in her that she wanted to follow a higher guidance. She discarded the coil and in a few days after the following period she conceived. She was not sure to start with, but when she missed her next period she was able, in hindsight, to reconstruct when the conception had happened, especially as her husband told her that the intense wish for a child had abruptly stopped since the presumed date of conception.

The experiences she had as an expectant mother completely changed her inner resistance into an affirmation full of respect and awe.

The embryonic stage as a phase of transformation influenced by higher, supersensible forces

Once it has been confirmed that a woman has entered the new condition of being pregnant, what I, as her gynaecologist, appeal to is an inner involvement with the individuality. If attention is paid to it this can lead to becoming acquainted with it very early on. Anyone who only undertakes an intellectual search for what mothers and doctors say about children in books, in the mass media or in direct reports, will be inundated with views and pathological conditions. Insecurity and fear increase to the same extent as this thirst for knowledge is satisfied. But the totally unique, first-time appearance of the descending individual can be found solely in the tender feelings of the mother herself. Once she becomes aware of it, it immediately brings about trust, courage and inner harmony on the level of mutual love.

Example:
These experiences had by a mother who has meanwhile had her third child is an illustration of this force of transformation towards inner maturity.

During her first pregnancy she had, on an intellectual level, acquired all the information she could possibly get hold of. Among catalogues of questions she kept meeting problems that had nothing in the slightest to do with her child. Each answer produced several new questions. The nervous state of this patient increased to the point of sleeplessness, until she eventually even had premature labour pains. My attempts to arouse her inner awareness only rarely succeeded. Thus the birth of her first child could not take place without fear, tension and ensuing (small) complications. Another pregnancy soon after this one was an important turning point. She let go more and more of the external aspects of the event and her intellectual questions about them, and discovered a growing relationship of love with the child. The birth, too, took place smoothly and with confidence. As the third child followed in quick succession the mother's inner maturity continued without a break. The sustaining power with which she devoted herself to her third relationship with the individuality of a child became for me a great experience. Only in rare cases have I seen as much empathy and trust in higher guidance as I observed in this mother.

If an expectant mother manages to make contact with the child then everything is accepted with confidence. She can pinpoint exactly what activities are good for her and which are not, and she can even feel that some activities considered unsuitable are not a strain and others which appear to be harmless are actually not beneficial.

One of my expectant mothers, to the indignation of some of the experienced older ladies in a tennis club, took it as a matter of course to continue to play tennis in her eighth month. Or there was another expectant mother who felt the highly recommended activity of swimming to be a strain. There is no acceptable standard of conduct for pregnant women! The unique character of the newly arriving human being determines the arrangements for the mother and child combination. It is always of great benefit to the expectant mothers when they come to realize that their feeling for the child's soul being is not experienced in the womb and the body of the embryo itself but that they feel the child's soul as a protecting being enveloping the maternal organism. The soul of the child is around the mother. The child's angel and the mother's angel work together at this protective sheath. Everyone who meets an expectant mother has a spontaneous feeling of wanting to treat her with deference and respect and protect her. Not until the moment of birth — with the first breath — does the sentient body (astral body) draw into the physical body. Sensation now becomes body-centred. For the first time the child's feeling is now as we visualize it to be with our everyday consciousness.

Even if the child is welcome, the first phase of pregnancy can often be oppressive. This is due to the clash of individualities. To begin with it is in the warmth of the maternal body that the child wants to settle down and start unfolding its life, but it also requires the inner, spiritual, loving warmth of the mother. If we compare this meeting of the two individualities with an outer encounter of two people, we can see that one person's needs can have the effect of calling up defensiveness in the other one. This process can bring about strong reactions in the metabolic system during the first two to three months of pregnancy (sickness and vomiting), and occasionally this reaction can be brought about in the maternal organism by the inherited forces of the child's father. In this case the overreaction would recur with each new pregnancy.

A picture helps some people understand this better. Imagine a person sitting at a desk concentrating on her work. Suddenly she notices that someone enters at the back of the room. She cannot see him, but she is aware of him and feels it disturbing her work. But turning round to find a visible solution to her problem produces no result. There is no escape from the feeling that someone is there. But there is no visible sign of him.

The only thing that can alter this situation is to accept this person selflessly, permitting the disturbance to take place or to show a higher kind of love. The mother has to adapt to the 'task' and recognize that total acceptance of this person is being asked for. Once the pregnancy is under way all the egoistic impulses give way to the overruling demands of the coming child. For the mother, pregnancy is an education in selflessness!

Whilst the first phase of becoming acquainted takes place on the ego level, the child now (until about the tenth week) enters more and more strongly into the realm of the mother's soul experience. Until about the fourteenth week of pregnancy she and the child breathe, feel and experience things as one. With the arrival of the fourth month the child's element of life also becomes a reality for the mother. Her abdomen suddenly grows beyond the usual size and she is aware of the slightest of movements. The child's movements can only really be explained physically from the fifth to sixth month onwards. When I hear more and more often that definite movements are ascertained as early as the twelfth to fourteenth week of pregnancy and the nature of this sensation continues to remain similar, we can conclude that a supersensible awareness of movements is on the increase. The movements are felt to be more like the quivering pulsations of the etheric. G.L. Flanagan describes the transition from one kind of movement to the other as a mechanical marionette-like vibration turning into a freer more individual way of moving.[6] Living pulsations like this are very familiar to a masseur who works with rhythms. He has to be capable of working together with them. The awareness of these movements in the womb assumes at some point more the quality of touching. Now the mother has consciously made contact with all the members of the child's being (about 18 to 22 weeks). From this point in its development onwards the child thrives in the whole complex of the mother's body. Now comes what is usually a very stable phase of pregnancy. The child's increase in growth is visible in the rising of the uterus above the navel and into the region of the ribcage, and there is a corresponding increase in the mother's weight. At about 28 weeks bodily maturity has completed its first stage. The ability to survive outside the womb is noticeably increasing.

The child works its way into the embryo in the reverse order to that of the members of its being (beginning with the etheric body and ending with the ego).

The beginning of the 'inner' birth

Whilst during the previous stage the child held no specific position in the the womb, it now begins to assume a spatial orientation to the earth. It establishes itself in the birth position, ideally with the head downwards. The growth of the part of the uterus spreading into the arch of the dia-phragm enables the mother to have intimate contact through her heart and lungs, the rhythmic centre of her organism. Superficially this phenomenon can cause dis-tress (breathlessness and palpitations). However, if the heart is trained to be an organ of perception then, when the child now makes the greatest physical demands on the mother's body, it can call up the last important act of unselfishness from the mother. The feeling of defensive-ness can be transformed into the final, most tender loving rounding off of the act of conception. With this 'conceiving in her heart' the mother can give the child the deepest gift of love at the beginning of its path towards being born into earthly life. If before conception there already existed an intimate connection with the child, which was then cher-ished further during pregnancy, this meeting of hearts can be a radical part of the mother-child relationship. These forces of its mother's love provide the birth phase with vital energy, and the mother's self-confidence peaks.

It is often stated that the child reacts very sensitively to certain influences in the environment, to people, and especially to the effect of technological and mechanical influences. Loudspeakers and TV images in particular provoke agitated defensive reactions. Everything going on in the realm of sound is also mirrored in the child's movement patterns. A rock tune excites, a Bach fugue calms the child, especially if heard live. These different ways of reacting lead many people to conclude that the child has a sensitive soul life of its own. But the child actually feels all this indirectly through the soul of its mother. If she is not aware of a finer feeling she can discover in the way the child behaves all that she herself has missed in her conscious feelings. Without the child she would remain unaware of all these perceptions. The unconscious part of her feeling life takes in far more than she dreams of. The child reacts to everything coming from her soul life.

In the same way as the fact of being open to and devoted to the child strengthens both the mother-child relationship and the child's development, so also on the other hand does it make it easier for the child to release itself and separate from the womb. The lowering of its position, the beginning of contractions, the opening of the uterus and the pushing out take place in harmony with cosmic rhythms and the child's will to enter earthly existence. As the child is released from the maternal organism the letting go is in the reverse order from which the child was received into the members of its mother's being. The closest connection, which was the physical one, is followed by a noticeable will to move taking place in the lowering of the position, a movement streaming and pushing downwards. The child's etheric body is pushing its way out and, with forces of suction, it draws the physical body along with it. The mother-to-be, who is intimately connected

with the child, and consciously aware of the inner processes taking place, is able to react with the proper
response to every variation in the flow of movement. Many
women, despite labour pains, feel that the moment of birth
has not yet begun, and would just as readily respond
immediately if they sensed the approach of birth despite
there not being any actual perceivable contractions.

Example:
I was once called to a home birth at four in the morning.
The patient had awoken, knew that her time had come, and
spontaneously sent me word. Not until after that did the
contractions really begin. When I arrived the birth was
already in full swing, and ten minutes later a girl was born.
The midwife only arrived at that moment. In this instance
the mother had dreamt both the name and the sex of her
daughter at the beginning of her pregnancy.

In another case the expectant mother waited six weeks
beyond the specified date of birth, yet there was no doubt
about it that the calculations were correct. With patience
and self-confidence the patient waited until her son was
born.

Birth

The child's appearance in the perceptible earthly world can make one aware of many of one's own supersensible experiences. As stated in the previous chapter the child's etheric body produces centrifugal movements perceptible to the mother. These exert on the physical body sucking forces which set the birth going at the right moment. The various members of the mother's being, working in harmony with the child, now spring into action. The astral body mediates the contractions that open up the birth canal and finally the contractions that push the child out. When the child arrives on earth the child's and the mother's individualities now meet in the sense world. How significant this moment of birth is for the individuality of the child can only be perceived spiritually. A human being's earthly life begins with a picture of that particular moment of the starry heavens of which the cosmic rhythms will, in the course of its life, offer it opportunities and possibilities for it as an individual. Rudolf Steiner tells us that the brain in the dome of the skull is an image of the world of the stars at the moment of birth.[7]

How differently the course of life has to run if, owing to manipulation of the moment of birth, a different position of the stars is stamped on the brain than the pre-destined one!

The actual length of time in the womb can vary in duration if the child's individuality requires it. As already mentioned, I have experienced an extreme overrunning by six weeks of the appointed date (because of early proof of pregnancy a mistake in the date was ruled out), without there being any sign of infection. And I have also experienced an extreme premature birth in the 32nd week, where the child's life forces were fully mature (needing neither intensive care nor incubator).

Example:
The first of these two patients had indicated that already during pregnancy she had a relationship of trust with her firstborn, and had also dreamt about him. She accepted all the stimuli which deepened her experience of the child in the light of these being real nourishment for her. She never doubted the rightness of what was happening, even when problems occurred. Therefore as the waiting time became longer and longer she adapted quickly to this difficult test of her patience. The effect she had on the people round her was like a firm rock holding its own among the breakers. Other people constantly urged her to take action, but she knew that everything was as it should be.

She wanted to have her child at home, but she lived a long way from my surgery. We agreed that if the child needed my assistance then it would be born at a suitable time. And that is what happened! I was called out early on a Saturday—a beautifully sunny day in autumn.

The birth was difficult. The head would not go in the proper direction, and despite good contractions no progress was being made. The expectant mother and her husband were exemplary. No complaints, no impatience. When the contractions suddenly stopped the midwife urged the use of something to stimulate them to start again. But this was the opportunity to allow the patient to rally her forces. The head was there, but remained too high up, and for half an hour she just walked to and fro. Then all of a sudden the contractions began again. Examination showed that the moment had come. With very few downward pushes she gave birth to a ten pound boy, who cried heartily and was rosy, and who showed not the slightest signs of being born too late. We were all aware that if it had not been for the patience and confidence of this mother and the substantial help of her husband we would not have been able to pull off this home birth. I attended this birth for eight hours, and I shall remember it as one of the finest ones I have ever experienced. I could feel only gratitude that I was privileged to be there.

Regard for the will of the child has to be rediscovered again in obstetrics after the long gap in which births have been programmed without any regard for this will. The only thing that can give us a proper relationship to birth is the overcoming of one-sided thinking in the sense realm, the material realm, and extending our view to the totality of body, soul and spirit. Anyone who can be present at a birth will always feel that there is a special mood there that is beyond an everyday one. The change taking place when, in the rhythm of reincarnation, a human being, through the process of birth, takes hold of its body to begin its human activity on earth gives us a glimpse of spiritual, super-sensible forces. We are aware that movements are passing from the higher members of this new earth citizen into its bodily existence. The mother and the father and all the other participants become involved in the experience. They are filled with feelings of joy, of wanting to forget themselves in devotion, love, deep commitment and a trusting awe, even if these are not qualities that come naturally to them. The great tension gripping them until the birth is completed gives way to a supportive, loving, harmonizing mood.

Modern obstetrics, of course, with all the aids laid on out of a one-sided materialistic approach, sometimes introduces clumsy obstacles to this salutary atmosphere. The more technical appliances are used and the more automatic application of medication takes place the less chance there is for the individual will of the child to play its part. This is not meant as a criticism of the progress made in modern obstetrics. We have no fault to find if there is a clear call for the skilful use of the most modern form of professional help.

If a participant at a birth has an empathetic way of thinking that is in accordance with the total nature of the child, that will contribute a framework that is meaningful and responsible. And the endeavour to create such an attitude of supportive awareness on the higher spiritual level is what this book is all about. To what a great extent the doctor can also be included in this occurrence can be seen in the following example of a home birth. This child introduced itself to me on a supersensible level.

Example:
It was Easter time, and I was called to a birth in the early hours of the morning. Shaken out of a deep sleep, I devoted a moment to gathering my mind, so that I could properly come to after the phone call. During this time I clearly saw a boy's face in front of me and was told what his name was. The boy part of the prediction was soon confirmed but not his name. So I did not tell my patient what I had experienced. A week later her husband came to me to get another birth certificate for the registrar, because the first one was out-of-date and therefore unacceptable. He added casually: 'It was quite a good thing actually, because we have changed the name!' They had changed it to the one I had heard!

When the birth begins the mother-child relationship goes through a decisive change. The baby pushes its way out of its maternal sheaths into this new, independent relationship to the earth—beginning with the head, the most individualized part of its body and the part that has been shaped the most by what has preceded this coming life. The mother supports this process with all her forces. In place of shielding and protecting the child inside her body she is now intent on letting go and separating physically. This must also be able to happen with inner awareness. Being able to make way for the child's greater independence provides the child with a step in its development similar to the significance of every phase of education until the child grows up.

A further important step in development — like 'a second breaking of the umbilical cord' — is the weaning process later on. This represents the strongest separating off of the child from the supporting strength of cosmic rhythms.

Deviations from the Ideal Picture of Pregnancy and Birth

Miscarriage

For those affected, a miscarriage is always seen as a sign of failure. Doubts grow regarding their capacity to have a healthy child. They cannot see it from the point of view of destiny because they cannot see the wider panorama opened up by an understanding of the supersensible aspect.

Example:
After having one healthy child a patient had two miscarriages. When she then, without any recognizable cause, lost a third child early on, this increased her doubt in herself. The thought forced itself upon her that she should not risk another pregnancy. In a conversation I had with her about the spiritual aspects of a miscarriage she told me about a dream she had had before the child miscarried. She could see the child clearly. It waved to her affectionately and said goodbye. But she could not understand why the child behaved as though they would see one another again soon. She did not take the dream very seriously. Not until we spoke about these spiritual connections and reincarnation could she arrive at an understanding of the dream. Then she had the courage and confidence again to have another pregnancy.

If we look for the causes of a miscarriage it is obvious that it would be our responsibility to look into all the physical factors and examine every possible treatment. The main causes of most miscarriages, however, are not in the physical dimension and can be guessed at only if we have a knowledge of the laws of reincarnation and karma. I have already given a description of life rhythms. Cosmic laws lead us to expect that the reincarnation rhythms of different human beings are just as individual as the various individualities themselves.

The lengths of a lifetime between birth and death are just as variable — and dependent on our destiny — as we are not interchangeable as individuals. If we extend earth existence to the moment of conception, even the shortest rhythms can be seen to be individually determined.

In the case of a miscarriage something always takes place karmically between the parents and the child. The mother always transfers to the child something from the earthly realm. This will have a strengthening effect on a new path of incarnation.

Indeed, there are patients who, through battling their way through the hard destiny of repeated miscarriages, arrive in the end at capacities they did not know they had, and with which they are able to give life to a following child. I will bring an account of a 31-year-old patient as an example.

Example:
After an abortion, which led to coming to grips with the most difficult of inner questioning, the situation opened up for a new possibility through her involvement with a new partner. Fear of becoming pregnant and feelings of guilt discouraged her altogether from being able to think of a future child. Several conversations about the various parts of human existence belonging together as a whole brought this patient finally to the point of taking the brave step of accepting a pregnancy which very soon ended in a miscarriage. It can well be imagined that at this point in time the old wounds broke open again and that she needed to undergo a new inner therapy. The next pregnancy was

again intentional, but it came to an end too after five months. Her connection with the child had already become very deep-seated and the pain of loss was therefore all the more intense. Renewed conversations to overcome this hurt transformed the patient this time into a person who was the nearest thing to a lioness defending her young. She became pregnant again, and this pregnancy ended in the seventh month because of an unavoidable burst bladder. The inner conviction that she was prepared to do anything for this child brought about a near miracle. The little creature which one would expect in the 'normal' way to be low in life forces had, despite being premature, as much vitality as a fully mature baby, and was able ten days later to go home from the clinic with her mother. It has become a radiant and healthy child.

The following is another instance of a struggle. It shows us what a tremendous responsibility we carry even as far as the various possibilities of treatment.

Example:
This young patient's pregnancy had in the first place to be saved by way of dialogue from ending in abortion. No sooner had the patient reached the firm resolve to keep the child when she began to bleed profusely. Despite it entailing the greatest privations she stayed resolutely in bed resting. For ten weeks she bled repeatedly, so that each time it was feared there would be a miscarriage. Measures to stop the bleeding, strong will-power, and a growing inner connection to the child helped each time to keep it alive. Once the second half of the pregnancy was reached there were no more difficulties at all. The patient had won the battle to have a healthy baby girl.

Premature birth

From the descriptions in the previous section it is obvious that a premature birth is governed by the same factors as a miscarriage. Only in this case the relationship between parents and child will have become firmer in an intimately physical way. So when a premature baby dies the separation is therefore more painful and leaves behind a greater feeling of grief (as with any death). Knowing, however, about the part of our existence that takes place in higher realms does help to overcome the pain of grief and transform it into forces of maturing.

If a premature baby survives we should always have in mind the child's desire to want to be born at a more favourable time than the calculated one. In later life one would hardly notice that the child had a difficult start in life.

Foetal death

The situation regarding a foetal death is that the physical remains cannot be pushed out of the maternal organism.

In the case of miscarriages and premature births the child arouses the premature pushing-out forces and therefore makes us wonder whether the child could live. With a foetal death the baby's life forces and will to incarnate are not sufficient for life. A weakness in the maternal organism may also play a part. The removing from the maternal organism usually needs the help of a doctor, because the individuality of the child has withdrawn from the process.

Early death of a child

Occasionally I also encounter the early death of a little child. What the pain of this loss means for the parents, especially for the mother, is usually so intense that nobody else can imagine it.

If there is no inner connection afterwards, the event can hardly be borne. If, however, the child is still experienced, astonishing new developments can arise.

A connection can be brought to life later through conversations about the other side of existence and the matter of the deceased child's destiny. In the following example the mother succeeded in quickly acquiring different kinds of thoughts of a higher kind, which helped her to make a new beginning.

Example:

A 33-year-old patient—expecting her third child—had to witness her second child, a child of three, being run over by a car and killed instantly. Judged by ordinary standards her behaviour to begin with was hardly conceivable. In a composed and straightforward manner she looked for an explanation of this stroke of destiny. Her first child was extremely difficult, whereas her second had been universally loved, always a ray of sunshine, like a little angel. And its death was similar. It lay there apparently unhurt, looking angelic. It had graciously accompanied us on a short stretch of its way and then returned to its heavenly existence so as to be able from then on to help its difficult older brother become more harmonious. After the death of its little sibling the first one had changed into a calm and loving child.

Children in Need of Special Care

One of the important questions today is that of children in need of special care. If there is no sense in handicapped human life—perhaps it is not even wanted by the individuality itself—should we therefore not reject it and eliminate it from our world? Is it possible for statistics to prove with greater certainty the probability that children in need of special care are more likely to come from pregnancies in the over-35s, and can these statistics get anywhere near an answer to the question of the human and social aspects of the destinies involved, and the actual intentions of the individuality concerned?

In the illuminating light shed by the thought of reincarnation quite different things can be said about both questions. If a need of destiny is the cause of a handicap that comes from before this life then we have a great responsibility to assist in helping this karmic balancing to come about. Anyone who has seen handicapped people in the hands of experienced anthroposophical curative teachers who are working out of a knowledge of the nature of such people does not need any theoretical explanations. He or she will be able to see the 'hidden' higher nature of the person glimmering through, as though longingly awaiting new opportunities in a new life and to be able to take an active part again in the goals of humankind. People of this kind reveal themselves in the active way they ray out love when they are given the proper guidance.

The second question can only arise if the human being cannot be seen as a living being who has freedom. Statistics apply best to statements about the unchanging, uniform, lifeless world. If a human being was that sort of robot, made up of many replaceable parts, then statistical statements about the phenomena of people in need of special care, or the arising of cancer, or any other problems to do with human destiny would be justified. However, the aspect of life and of freedom and the unique nature of human individuality certainly rules out the suitability of any statistical survey regarding people's future. If I personally were to draw up statistics out of my experience as a gynaecologist regarding the question of children in need of special care born to mothers over 35 — which I would be extremely reluctant to do — I would arrive at a statement that would contradict modern science. In almost 20 years of activity as a doctor I have had to do with numerous handicapped children. Today I still have to see my first mother over 35 who has a handicapped child. The oldest patient I have had who had a child in need of special care was aged 34. This statement is of no scientific value because I have always worked only with individual people with their unique destinies belonging in their particular predestined social environment. Statistics are an unsuitable instrument for understanding individualities.

From the point of view of reincarnation and karma a further important connection must be included which has already been mentioned regarding this problem. A conception does *not* happen primarily on the basis of the parents' volition but is always instigated by the unborn soul itself. The wish to have children is encouraged by the child to make the parents feel ready to have physical union so that conception can take place. All the parents can do is to prepare themselves to be willing to take on future responsibility in an unselfish way to care for a human being between the time of conception and becoming a grown-up. It is the child itself, with the help of higher spiritual beings, who chooses the moment of birth, the place and the social setting for its earthly life. It could happen that a couple at the end of their 40s could be just right for the individual destiny of a particular child. But the prevalent opinion today, which almost everyone sub-scribes to, forbids the realization of such a destiny. 'What would other people say, the neighbours, our relatives or our grown-up children, if we had another child!' I often hear such comments as a reason for discussing contra-ception at their time of life.

How naturally a 42-year-old mother took to her Dominic can be found in another part of this book (pp. 26–7).

When we also hear Rudolf Steiner telling us that generations before birth a future earth citizen sees his ancestors and then finally his parents way ahead at the end of the series, our superficial, intellectual considerations on this matter can appear very poverty-stricken.

The matter of abortions, which has already been aired, also acquires in this light quite different dimensions.

If we succeed in helping parents to understand the sig-nificance of a handicapped incarnation in the light of the evolution of the whole of humankind, most of them will show a willingness to go along with it. They are prepared to trust and accept their destiny.

The prevalent opinion about handicaps, however, especially Down syndrome, appears so terrible to many people that they fight shy of forming an opinion of their own and prefer to choose the 'safe' way of not having any more children.

We should also distinguish between the various dis-abilities. Not until parents actually go through with it will they find out how rewarding it can be to live with a child in need of special care. Only in hindsight can they see how their own development has benefited and can become especially aware of the opportunity it has afforded for giving the being of the child the best foundations for pre-paring for a future life without impediment.[8]

Pregnancy in the phase after the mother is 35 has today

become a legal plaything. It can sometimes even lead to legal consequences if the doctor neglects to tell the expectant mother of the possibility of handicap and amniocentesis. The doctor is held responsible for the occurrence of a substandard life, and neither the parents nor the State can be burdened with the upkeep. An understanding of handicap on the basis of reincarnation makes the problem fairly and squarely a matter for the parents' individual decision. If they would accept a child in need of special care then it is unnecessary to have the foetal fluid analysed. In the case of mothers who nevertheless want such a clarification they have to realize that if there is a genetic deviation they would have to agree to an abortion, despite the fact that the child is usually already moving in the womb. By then the inner connection to it is already deep-rooted, and if it has to be forcibly removed it is an almost insurmountable emotional strain. Besides, once the child has been born it is far easier to accept a handicap than it is during pregnancy!

If during pregnancy or in the course of the birth damage is done to the child through external influences, this can also lead to disability (e.g. spastics, behavioural disturbances caused by a shock to the mother in early pregnancy, thalidomide children). It is not so simple to answer the question whether here, too, destiny plays its part in individual cases, especially where the parents are concerned. Taking care of a child like this in any case lays highly demanding claims on human responsibility, and it is a tremendous maturing process for the people who take it on.

The Question of Abortion

What anthroposophy has to say to people wanting an abortion

The question of abortion is a typical 'problem' arising after 'uncontrolled' sexual relations. On this subject, too, there have been articles written from the anthroposophical point of view (Debus, Hoffmeister).

What can anthroposophy contribute as a solution to the question of abortion in direct dealings with the persons concerned?

People who are thinking of having an abortion can often arrive at a change of heart and the willingness to continue with the pregnancy if they can hear a clear exposition of the following aspects of life.

Human life takes place in an individual rhythm over repeated earthly lives. Body-free existence between death and a new birth is just as valid a part of human existence as the existence we know of with our earthly senses that takes place between birth and death.

When human beings are ready to incarnate they experience strong forces of attraction towards their future earthly body. This is based on an archetypal image which human beings themselves have constructed in creative activity with the help of the highest spiritual hierchies. At conception this archetype unites with the fructified ovum in the mother. On this basis the very first beginnings of a human being in the womb must be regarded as a valid human being. The removal of the beginnings of a human earthly existence has to mean the same thing as killing a person after birth. If we add to these ideas thoughts about connections of destiny between various people, especially those between the parents and children which were begun in earlier lives, this at the very least gives strong pointers to look at things in a different way. The abortion question is lifted onto a different level. One begins to see the possibility of a whole human individuality hidden in every pregnancy.

It is very seldom that these ideas meet with a totally negative response. They are understood, though often not taken up sufficiently into the forces of the heart. Now and again personal trouble weighs so heavily that the positive reactions of the heart cannot rise above them. With logical arguments about one's apparent goals in life, the intellect strangles the truth that is beginning to dawn on the heart. It is not an easy thing to trust the heart as a 'sense organ for spiritual truths', which can become fully fledged knowledge if one lets it reach the thinking. The decision to fall back on abortion, which is seen as being the only possible solution to the problem, is a misjudgement. The desire is there to return to the feelings that existed before, of being totally secure. The truths understood by the head and recognized as truth are regarded as not realizable, and produce fear and a feeling of unease. People put forward strange arguments to make themselves feel outwardly secure: 'Despite all this I shall have to have an abortion because I have still to finish my exams (in six months' time), after that I would accept a child.' Or: 'My father is a strict Catholic! He rigorously rejects the disgrace of having a child before marriage and would throw me out of the family.'

Short-term peace of mind coupled with long-term emotional problems is preferred to short-term difficulties coupled with long-term emotional health, and not only when it is a matter of a stroke of fate in the form of an 'unwanted child'.

Soul weakness (depression and weakness of will) can lead to the decision to have an abortion, if the whole aim of the conversation was to come to an agreement regarding continuing with the pregnancy, but the whole social circumstances of the mother-to-be can play their part too. Gratifyingly it often happens, and increasingly so, that the people who do see reason always go through astonishing development with their child. It has never happened to me that a patient with whom the conversation produced a happy outcome regretted the decision later. On the contrary, all of them have afterwards expressed their heartfelt thanks for the possibility of undreamt of inner transformation, as the following examples show.

Example:
A 28-year-old patient of mine, on breaking up with her partner, discarded the coil she had only been using for a short time. She wanted to be free of it because she did not need it any more. She made light of a suggestion on my part that destiny might suddenly introduce a new partner which could very quickly lead to a pregnancy, which might even be prompted by a child that wanted to come. Three months later the patient came to me about a pregnancy arising through a chance encounter with a partner, and she was determined to have an abortion. The lack of commitment to the partner, her career and the threatened loss of her independence made it impossible to consider having a child. A conversation about the spiritual/soul aspects of our existence considerably altered her attitude to a child. After thinking about it for a few days she decided to carry the child full term, possibly giving it out to adoption. This pregnancy proved a turning point in her life. Her inner development acquired quite new possibilities and her life was enriched with new values. A great many practical activities which she found deeply satisfying developed out of this in course of time. And she kept the child. Looking back later at the change that had taken place

in her she became more and more grateful that she had come to a real understanding of her destiny at the time.

Example:
Another patient, a very young one of 17, who had tried the symptothermal method but not applied it conscientiously, came to see me at the surgery with her mother who was also a patient of mine. She was pregnant and she thought it would be a straightforward matter to get me to sign a request for her to have an abortion. She took quite naturally to a broadening of her view to include further aspects of human existence, but her mother had grave doubts. However eventually her mother came round to supporting her daughter's wish to have the child. This event is now five years past. After the birth of the baby the patient married and has meantime had a further much-wanted child. Her relatives were very critically disposed to start with, but they changed their attitude even before the baby was born. After the baby arrived nobody in her happy family or the social environment doubted that she had done the right thing.

Example:
A 42-year-old patient with four children, two already over 20, and herself divorced, was expecting a baby by another man who was married, and whose marriage was otherwise stable. In addition to this her economic situation was thoroughly unclear; she was practically destitute. She was actually in the course of setting up her own business. According to today's manner of assessing, here was a situation which for more reasons than one would justify an abortion. As well as the social embarrassment of the complicated circumstances of the partner, there seemed little prospect of being able to include the child in a family situation, and finally her age, at which she could even have a handicapped child. All these things left no room for

doubt. The emotional life of the patient was also badly affected. Nevertheless the course of the conversation led clearly to a decision to have the baby. The consequences of this positive decision could not have been foreseen logically. On the birth of the child, who was heartily loved and cared for by the other children, an ideal living possibility presented itself to the patient as though by 'chance', which the patient has been taking splendid advantage of right until today. According to her relatives the child was always the family's little ray of sunshine, the focus of their love. There was never any more doubt of the rightness of taking on the destiny of having this child.

I could add many more such examples. But may these few suffice to show that on the one hand trust in the wise guidance of spiritual beings and, on the other hand, courage to do the right thing can always help anyone to move forward in their development. As a gynaecologist I personally am grateful to be privileged to witness such changes in the course of a destiny. A very important part in the care of women with unwanted pregnancies certainly is that one not only motivates them to keep the unborn child, but that one arranges help for them at any time so that they can reshape their lives anew. If the patients feel the genuine nature of the wish to help them, they will soon acquire a good relationship to their child. If this support is not forthcoming, or if it is not offered sincerely, these people will not accept the child fully. Often a permanent resentment lingers on. This pattern is unnecessary; yet today it is taken as an indicator pointing to the advisability of abortion.

An unwanted pregnancy as a life opportunity

Every patient I have experienced has later on confirmed that keeping the child was the sensible thing to do, in fact the only thing possible. They also always acquired the insight that they had undergone important experiences and transformation. Most of them soon realized, too, that to come successfully through a time of hard testing is more rewarding than avoiding facing up to the problem. The above examples are a confirmation of this!

The significance of the social environment

If, in the immediate circle of someone expecting an unwanted child, there is no one willing to support her, then she will need to have enormous courage to go through with it. Occasionally individual conversations appear to be sufficient to preserve the child's life. But if pressure from the social environment to get rid of it is too much to bear, the pregnant woman will resign herself to her fate and the child will be the victim. This produces a distinct weakening of self-confidence. Sometimes the people involved are of the opinion that nobody else is going to accept the child, and that support is unlikely to be forthcoming. Then comes the unexpected surprise—relatives do considerably more about the new turn of events that was ever expected.

Abortion and the doctor's involvement

Few women asking for abortions are fully aware of the part played by the doctor who performs the operation. This human dilemma is a twofold challenge for the gynaecologist. His consent to the abortion and the manner in which it is done have both to be considered. The doctor is, after all, considerably more karmically connected with the child about to be killed than the mother asking for the abortion.[9] The doctor can either alternate between being the judge and the executioner or be both at once. That is, he bears the main responsibility, and can only do it justice if he faces up to what he is doing and challenges the expectant mother with convincing counter-arguments. Anyone who can include the picture of the human being's whole being of spirit, soul and body in their idea of reincarnation will hardly find an abortion acceptable, of course. The expectant mother's individual decision to have an abortion can in the last resort not be prevented from happening – the same as with any human misconduct permitted by law. The doctor can, however, from out of his own inner conviction, do justice to his feeling of responsibility, so as not to have to be either a judge or an executioner. He can – because he recognizes it as *his own* spiritual truth not to approve of abortions – refuse to give his signature of consent, and most certainly not carry out the act of destroying a human being. An abortion can anyway hardly be fitted into the picture of a doctor as a 'healer'. An unwanted pregnancy is not an illness. A doctor's profession is to cure illnesses and not to do away with life and create illnesses.

Modern Technologies as Applied to the Beginning of Human Life on Earth

Artificial insemination[10]

A procedure is developing which, a few decades ago, could hardly have been imagined. And this is not only that a human being can be 'created' by means of a technical procedure outside the female body (in a test tube) but that it can also be reared technologically outside the body. Premature babies are already being kept alive successfully from the twenty-third week.

The idea that this is technically feasible will be followed by the idea that it is also possible to bridge the gap, without there being a womb, between the stage where the cells begin to multiply and the stage of a premature baby including the phase of birth.

This approach seems to suggest that our view of existence does not look beyond what is soluble on a material, technical level. More far-reaching concepts could become superfluous.

Modern materialistically orientated medical technology presents us with a bleak picture of the human being, one in which people will be utterly uniform, for the individual free spirit will disappear more and more.

One single anthroposophical thought is sufficient to raise doubts that the spiritual/soul development of an individual could take the form of a technologically existing robot. Which supersensible members would the technologically created child unite with, if there are no human maternal sheaths?

In order to recognize and redeem this technological entity we shall have to create in ourselves, as a counterforce, the spiritual/soul images of the human being that support the independent individual.

The characteristics of gene technology

This process carries the previous developments even further. On the basis of the mental attitude behind the materialistically orientated theory of heredity the manipulation of a human being's bodily attributes can be indefinitely extended. The process will be determined by expediency. With the intention merely of eliminating hereditary illnesses human beings will ultimately be made an instrument for economic interests.

It is unlikely that there is any chance of halting these developments any more. But there could be a sufficient number of free individualities in the world who, through the creation of a living picture in ourselves built up of spirit, soul and body, and of living thoughts of pre-existence and reincarnation, would endeavour to muster counter-forces of healing.

Postscript

For many years now people have been telling me about experiences parents-to-be have been receiving from children not yet born. People spoke about dream experiences, about hearing the child's name, about very delicate yet very real relationships between mothers and their unborn children. These accounts, told to me humbly and with reservation, moved me very deeply, and from then on I looked at children with quite different eyes. There arose in me quite naturally a feeling of reverence towards the world out of which the child's being comes, and this feeling grew ever stronger. When a number of children were born into my own family, and my wife told me about the dream experiences she had in connection with the ones we were expecting, I was very happy to be privileged to be involved in this.

The idea of making a systematic collection of such reports and spreading the message as widely as possible came to me around 1978 when discussions were in progress regarding paragraph 218. Soon a large number of reports of experiences in connection with articles in periodicals and even actual encounters were compiled, some of which are included here.

While these things were being collected a close contact arose with one or another person, until finally the cooperation came about with Max Hoffmeister and Hartmut Goerg which then led to the present book.

Max Hoffmeister has been actively engaged for decades with the natural scientific-foundations of incarnation, and has been working to broaden these views by including anthroposophical insights. Two books of his on subjects related to this theme have already been published.[1] Hartmut Goerg's profession as an anthroposophical gynae-cologist gives him the opportunity of meeting with a lot of cases in which women often have to make distressing decisions. With the help of spiritual-scientific knowledge of human development he has been able to give many women advice that offers more than the conventional kind, and helps them through great emotional pressure. What he is able to contribute has sprung from a background of a great deal of medical experience.

First and foremost our very special thanks go to our chief contributors, namely, those who have told us of their experiences and released them for publication. In particular Frau Cordelia Boettcher and Frau Dr Alberty have given me valuable help in compiling these reports. Herr Willhelm Gaedecke, from whose collection I was permitted to use some accounts given by children, and all those people whose advice and help made the existence of this book possible are also heartily included in my thanks.

The authors would gratefully welcome it if the present book were to call forth further accounts of experiences. The publishers will be glad to forward contributions.

Dietrich Bauer

Notes

Dietrich Bauer, 'I want to be born now!'

1. From a lecture by Prof. Dr Petersen, given at the Academy for Further Education in Medicine in Bad Segeberg on 5 December 1981, on the theme of our responsibility and paragraph 218, or how do we respond to the human being in its pre-birth condition (included in the periodical *Wahrnehmungen*, issued by the Association for the Advancement of Therapy).
2. Quoted from O.J. Hartmann, medical/pastoral psychology.
3. The Lily family (lily, amaryllis, iris) belong to the plants that are monocotyledons or plants with leaves that have parallel veins. When the seed of this plant group germinates the root which forms first soon withers and is replaced by a relatively weak root from the shoot. This is the opposite of the way the dicotyledons behave, that is, the plants with cross-veined leaves (this group includes all blossoming plants with the exception of this first-mentioned group). With these, the primary root often develops into a taproot, thus bringing about a deep connection with the earth. The way the root forms and then withdraws again expresses a 'reluctance' in this family of plants to connect firmly and permanently with the earth. The bulb that then forms is an organ that makes the plant very independent of the changes in the earth's environment, such as dryness, cold and heat. The simple unformed leaf (no regular subdivision, no shaping of the edges) is comparable to the lowest part of leaf formation of the dicotyledons. In the course of metamorphosis the green blossom case arises out of the foliage, and then the calyx and the inner organs of the blossom — the petals and stamens. You can therefore think of the leaf of the monocotyledons as the sepal of the dicotyledons. To put it simply: the lily-related plants are chiefly of a blossom nature.

    The ring of blossom itself is constructed strictly on the

number three (twice three petals, twice three stamens, forming a cross). They form a regular six-pointed star. This form
demonstrates the forces of the expanses surrounding the
earth, which also for example come to expression in the six-
pointed stars on which snowflakes are constructed.

Thus the lily (and those plants related to it) is rightly a
symbol for such beings as newborn children, who come down
to earth from the far reaches of the cosmos. Jakob Boehme
(1575–1624) wrote: 'The lily branch shows the newborn spirit
as a proper image of God.'

In the rose we have a symbol of those beings who have
united with the earth. It roots deeply, is a hardy perennial
through the solidity of its woody formation, and does not
blossom until it has established itself. The leaves are regularly formed (pinnate, serrated). The Rose family covers
fruit-forming herbaceous perennials and trees (pear, quince,
raspberry, strawberry, and the apple too, the symbol of
earthly knowledge). The blossom is constructed on a five-
pointed star. The pentagram is an ancient symbol expressing a connection at the highest level between heaven and
earth.

4. Max Hoffmeister says to this that an angel is just as real a
being as an ego, the spiritual core of a human being, our
individuality. All human beings have a guardian angel who
knows all about them, shares their feelings and sufferings and
also perceives their thoughts. Therefore angels have an astral
body and an etheric body as human beings do, but no
physical, material body. Their astral bodies, however, do not
harbour egoistic drives and passions as do those of human
beings, but are filled with selfless devotion, a desire to help
and humility. Their astral bodies are actually what human
beings' astral bodies will be like when they have been fully
purified and have therefore become angelic. This stage is
called Spirit Self (Manas). Every effort we make to purify our
soul life brings us nearer to our angel, and the better he can
help us. (See Christian Morgenstern: *Der Engel spricht von
seinen Leiden* — The Angel Speaks of his Suffering.)

All the pictures of angels, especially at the beginning of the modern age, go to show the need people felt to make an image of angels. The important thing is not what an angel actually looks like, whether they have wings or what these would look like, and so on. Basically the only thing that matters is that we approach him, our guardian angel, by way of some sort of depiction, so that we can address him personally. After all, it is he who is always with us, accompanying us from one earthly life to the other. It is very helpful for us earthly human beings if we can learn in this way to experience a real relationship to him. We sense that our angel responds to us, because he expects this of us and actually needs the human being to be aware of him.

If we bear in mind that he accompanies us from earthlife to earthlife, and therefore knows all there is to know of our past, our present and what our destiny holds for our future, then we can have a feeling, too, of how expectant and anxious an angel is when he accompanies the human being who has been entrusted to him into a new incarnation. And at his back, actually entering into him, is the helping presence of the archangel Gabriel, as we can sense in the way it was depicted in the sixteenth century.

In the Gospels the angel accompanies the human being at conception (at the annunciation of both John and Jesus), and in the hour of Jesus' birth the angel appears to the shepherds in the field. In the *Sistine Madonna* Raphael opens one more time the curtain in front of the spiritual world with its many angel faces. Then the curtain closed again until, in Christ's hour of death, the curtain is torn asunder in the temple. In the transition from life to death the angel world again becomes visible; in the Garden of Gethsemane an angel gives strength to Jesus in his death agony (Luke 22:44), and there appeared an angel unto him from heaven, strengthening him, and angels appear to the women at the empty tomb. Thus the angel world is visible to the seeing soul both at life's beginning and at its end. It is right that we visualize angels as real spiritual beings.

5. Rudolf Steiner, *Okkulte Untersuchungen über das Leben zwischen Tod und never Geburt* (20 lectures, 1912–13).

Bibliography:

The New Testament, in Emil Bock's translation

Karl Koenig, *Brothers and Sisters, The Order of Birth in the Family*

G.E. Lessing, *Die Erziehung des Menschengeschlechtes* (The education of the human race), 1780

Rudolf Steiner, *Theosophy, an introduction to the supersensible knowledge of the world and the destination of man*

— *Wo und wie findet man den Geist?* (Where and how do we find the spirit?), 18 public lectures, Berlin 1908/09, GA 57

— *Geisteswissenschaftliche Menschenkunde* (Spiritual-scientific study of man), 19 lectures, Berlin 1908/09, GA 107

— *Manifestations of Karma*

— *Between Death and Rebirth*, ten lectures, Berlin 1912/13, GA 141

— *Der Tod als Lebenswandlung* (Death as life transformed), seven lectures 1917/18, GA 182

— *Man's Being, His Destiny and World Evolution*, seven lectures, Christiania (Oslo) 1923, GA 226

Max Hoffmeister, Human nature — prebirth — reincarnation

1. Text taken from Michael Debus, *Die Reform des §218*, Stuttgart 1978.

2. Erich Blechschmidt, *Sein und Werden. Die menschliche Fruehentwicklung* (Being and Becoming. A human being's early development), Stuttgart 1982.

3. See illustration in *Die Genesis in der menschlichen Embryonalentwicklung* (Genesis in the embryonic development of a human being), by Kaspar Appenzeller, Zbinden Publishing Co, Basel 1976, p. 56.

4. More about this in *Die uebersinnliche Vorbereitung der Inkarnation* (Supersensible preparation for incarnation) by Max Hoffmeister, Die Pforte, Basel 1979, pp. 73–81 with illustration.

5. See illustrations in *abc-Biologie*, Harry Deutsch Verlag, Frankfurt am Main 1968, pp. 282ff.

6. The Graz biologist Otto Julius Hartmann in his *Dynamische Morphologie*, Klostermann Verlag, Frankfurt am Main 1959, pp. 60–1, divides human embryonic development into three sections: the pre-embryonic stage until about day 16, the actual development of the embryo from day 17 until the end of the second month, and the development of the foetus from the beginning of the third month onwards.

7. The Greek word *aner, andros* = man (andreas = male) and gynē, gynaika = woman (as in gynaecology = study of women's illnesses).

8. By the seventh week the embryo is about 1.8 cm long; it has already assumed the human form when sexual differentiation in the position of the interior genitals begins. See Wolfgang Schad, *Die Vorgeburtlichkeit des Menschen* (The prebirth state of the human being), Stuttgart 1982, p. 52.
   The penis does not protrude until the end of the eighth week.

9. Erich Blechschmidt, *Die vorgeburtlichen Entwicklungsstadien des Menschen* (The various stages of a human being before birth), Karger Verlag, Freiburg 1960, p. 223, figs. 142 and 143.

10. In the case of anthropoids it is of course two to three years later, as monkeys are altogether halfway between humans and mammals.

11. Friedrich Kluge, *Etymologisches Woerterbuch der deutschen Sprache* (Etymological dictionary of the German language), 1934, p. 555.

12. See for example Menge-Guethlings, *Griechisches Woerterbuch*.

13. The Greek psyche = soul, *soma* = body, in the sense of a living, ensouled body rather than *sarx* = flesh.
    Jakob von Uexkuell (1864–1944), *Streifzuege durch die Umwelten von Tieren und Menschen – Ein Bilderbuch unsichtbarer Welten – Bedeutungslehre*, rde 13 (Incursions through the environments of animals and human beings – a picture book of invisible worlds – study of meanings).

Arthur Jores, *Vom kranken Menschen* (About sick people). A textbook for doctors, Georg Thieme Verlag, Stuttgart.

Thure von Uexkuell (born 1908), *Grundfragen der psychosomatischen Medizin*, rde 179/180, 1965 (Basic questions of psychosomatic medicine).

14. Norbert Lebert, *Psychopotenz*, in the chapter 'Die Faust im Magen', Bertelsmann, 1969.

15. Josef Rattner, *Psychosomatische Medizin heute – seelische Ursachen koerperlicher Erkrankungen* (Psychosomatic medicine today – emotional causes of bodily illnesses), chapter 7, 'Das Magen- und Zwoelffingerdarmgeschwuer' (Stomach ulcers and duodenal ulcers), Werner Classen Verlag, 1964.

16. As we know, at baptism the child is called by its name, the human being as it were being called into the body. We are already told this in the Old Testament in the Book of Judges 13:24, 'And the woman bore a son and *called* his name Samson.'

17. The task of drugs would then be solely to diminish psychically based impediments which appear physically, so that the mental element has easier access. Therefore a stomach operation would only make sense if it is at least going to be followed by treatment on the mental/emotional level.

18. For more about this see Max Hoffmeister, *Reincarnation – Antwort auf das Raetsel des Menschen? – Einfuehrung in den Gedanken der wiederholten Erdenleben* (Reincarnation – the answer to the riddle of man? – An introduction to the thought of repeated earth lives), Achberg Verlag, 1984, p. 286(1).

19. To the ancient Greeks a daemon meant a divine being, one of the lower gods. A genie, one that brought good luck, they called a good daemon, and one that brought harm a bad daemon. In the Bible only those who do harm are called demons, namely, devils, spirits (a change of meaning due to the limiting of a concept which was originally broader), shadows and ghosts. The original meaning of *daimōn* however, was the will of the gods, fate (e.g. *kata daimona* = according to divine providence; *pros daimona* = counter to the

will of the gods; *syn daimoni* = with the help of God; *en daimoni* = in God's hand). *Daimon* derives etymologically from *daimonai* = I allot, *dai* = to allot, sanskrit, *dātrám* = what is allotted, etc.; according to ancient usage *daimonia* means that which is allotted by the gods, one's allotted fate.

20. The German word *Mensch* (= human being) derives from the Indo-Germanic root 'men' from which many word formations are derived in all the Indo-Germanic languages. This 'men' means ultimately 'to be spiritually stimulated', also 'to think, consider'. More about this in Hoffmeister, op. cit., pp. 277–9).

21. Popper and Eccles, *Das Ich und sein Gehirn* (The I and its brain), Piper Verlag, 1982.

22. Also in Mark 14:38; and in another version in John 6:63, 'It is the spirit that quickeneth (*zoopoioun* = creating soul life). The flesh profiteth nothing.'

23. We have to distinguish the Gnostics from the Gnosticists whose teaching was very widespread, especially in the first two centuries in early Christian times. Among the so-called early Christians in particular, before they became the established Church (AD 324), Gnosis was the philosophical foundation of knowledge (the Logos theory); see more on this in *Esoterisches Christentum* by Gerhard Wehr, Ernst Klett Verlag, 1975, pp. 74ff.

24. The Jews who, since the Babylonian captivity, lived widely dispersed (Diaspora, see John 7:35) in Asia Minor and Egypt did not in the end understand Hebrew any more, but spoke the widespread Greek language which, since Alexander the Great, had become the accepted language of civilization, the *Koinē* (general public) of the Hellenistic age. Therefore, so we are told, 72 scholars, six out of each of the twelve tribes of the Israelite peoples, were authorized, as early as the fourth century BC, and independently of one another to start with, to translate the five books of Moses (the Pentateuch, the Torah) from Hebrew into Greek. This Greek translation was later on called, in Latin, *Septuaginta(duo)*, i.e. seventy(two).

25. If we were to understand this to mean the human spirit came

forth from the spirit of God, as we can read in Genesis 1:26 ('And God said, Let us make man [*poiesomen, poiesis,* from which comes poetry, etc.] in our image, after our likeness') then it is a matter of the Godhead creating the human being spiritually. And this is how people must have originally understood it, as we can see from the sculptures on the gable of the north portal of Chartres Cathedral: 'Adam as the thought of God'. Not until the second account of creation from Genesis 2:5ff does it speak of the physical creation of man.

26. *Aristoteles' Hauptwerke,* compiled, translated and introduced by Wilhelm Nestle, Alfred Kroener Verlag, Stuttgart 1938.

27. Think of the description in Luke 1: 39–45 where Mary comes to Elisabeth. In verse 41 it says ... when Elisabeth heard the salutation of Mary the babe (*brephos,* now in the sixth month, according to verse 36) leapt in her womb. A woman reported that during her first pregnancy she repeatedly felt the urge to go into every cathedral and church. And in the Church of Our Lady in Munich she felt a powerful movement coming from the child whom she had carried beneath her heart for three months.

28. Geraldine Lux Flanagan, *Die ersten neun Monate des Lebens* (The first nine months of life), Rowohlt-Sachbuch 6605.

29. For instance A. Dermott, *Zytogenetik des Menschen und anderer Tiere* (The cytogenics of human beings and of other animals), Gustav Fischer Verlag, 1977. See also Hoffmeister, *Die uebersinnliche Vorbereitung der Inkarnation,* pp. 69, 91, 111).

30. The Gotting Professor Gerhard Heberer, well known in scientific circles and who wrote *Die Evolution der Organismen,* expressed the basic problem in 1950 as follows. Is organic development planned or is it sheer chance? Is the multiplicity of human life the deliberate aim of a guiding power at the primal core of the world or the consequences of a complex of chance factors strung together haphazardly in the course of the history of the earth and of life? According to his view, the mutations can be regarded as a kind of accident which the chromosomes meet with from time to time. On the

whole, evolution is based on an enormous complex of chance happenings.

31. Incidentally this is the Hebraic *manna* which the children of Israel were given on their way from Egypt through the desert (Exodus 16:13ff.; 31–5; Numbers 11:6–9; Deuteronomy 8:3 and 16; Joshua 5:12, etc.). Exodus 16:15, 'This is the bread (manna) which the Lord hath given you to eat.' In John 6:31 it says: 'Our fathers did eat manna in the desert [desert, *eremos* in Greek is an image for solitude and hence as derived from the Latin word *eremita* = hermit]'; verse 35: 'And Jesus said unto them: I am the bread of life [zoē].' In Indo-Germanic, manna = spirit, in Hebrew manna = gift (from heaven), but this is the very spirit which human beings should take up into themselves.

32. Hugo S. Verbrugh, *Wiederkommen. Erfahrungen des Vorgeburtlichen und der Reinkarnationsgedanke* (Return. Experiences from before birth and the idea of reincarnation), Stuttgart 1982.

33. When at the age of twelve the author was given an anaesthetic (chloroform) to have his septic appendix removed he also experienced a spiral. From out of the centre of this shining golden spiral something like a small shuttle moved along the curves and shot out at the end. After a while it returned and rolled down the curves of the spiral back to the centre. When it had arrived there the little patient awoke. That would have been a kind of 'real' dream picture, first of all of the excarnating process and then of the incarnating process, of coming to himself again on entering the body.

34. In Matthew 26:41 it says, in Luther's translation: 'The spirit indeed is willing, but the flesh is weak'. However a literal translation from the original Greek text would be: 'The spirit (*pneuma*) is an onward-driving force (*prothymon*), but the body (*sarx, sarcos* = flesh) has no strength of its own (*asthenēs* = weak, asthenic).' The spirit, however, is divine, is something that fills us with enthusiasm (*en* = in, *theos* = God, i.e. the divine force in us). The spirit is caught up by the body,

the blood is stirred into motion, and in the life of the soul it can become conscious of itself.

35. The title of the book The Tatian Gospel Harmony: *Das Evangelium des vollkommenen Lebens* (The Gospel of the perfect life), Humata Verlag Harold S. Blume.

36. The Apocrypha to the New Testament.

37. Richard Karutz, *Das Menschenbild in der Weisheit der Voelker* (The image of man in folk wisdom), student material for the study of ethnology, Verlag Die Kommenden, Freiburg 1963 (out of print).

38. Ibid., p. 270.

39. Quoted up to here from Peter Petersen, *Retortenbefruchtung und Verantwortung* (Retort fertilization and responsibility), Verlag Urachhaus, Stuttgart 1985, p. 108.

40. That plant models are connected with the etheric world is demonstated by the famous apocalypse tapestries of Angiers.

41. A much abbreviated version of M. Hoffmeister's (see note 4, pp. 97–100), which was taken from Andreas Lommel's *Die Unambal – Ergebnisse der Frobenius Expedition of 1938/39 nach NW Australien* (The Unambal – results of the Frobenius Expedition of 1938/39 to NW Australia), private printing of the Museum for Ethnic Studies, Hamburg 1952 (lent out by university libraries).

42. Kamaloka means the sphere which is otherwise called the region of soul purification after death, or purgatory.

43. a) Wilfried Noelle: *Woerterbuch der Religionen* (Dictionary of religions), Goldmann Verlag, 642/643 – notes: Hinduism pp. 195–6, soul migration pp. 368–9.
    b) Heimo Rau, *Indien's Erbe* ... (India's heritage) p. 36, Verlag Freies Geistesleben.
    c) M. Hoffmeister (see note 17, pp. 9, 249ff, 258ff, 287, and note 4, p. 301).

44. Ewhe negroes: see Pamphylier Er in Plato's *Politeia*, X13–16 (RK 27)/27a, 614–621b, pp. 304–10. See also Hoffmeister (note 17, pp. 147ff).

45. See Hoffmeister (note 4, pp. 142 and 146).

46. See Hoffmeister (note 18, pp. 34–5). Names that point to

future intentions are for example: Alexander (Greek) = a defender and protecter of men; Andreas (Greek) = a manly person; Arthur (Celtic) = with the strength of a bear; Cornelius (Latin) = as strong and firm as a horn (*cornu*), also Cornelia; Dionysius (Greek) = dedicated to the god Dionysos; Gudrun (Germanic name of a Valkyrie) = proclaiming wisdom in battle; Edith = a fighter for inheritance (this was a the name of the wife of Otto I, who descended from Anglo-Saxon royalty). Lit. Ernst Wasserzieher, *Hans und Grete*, Ferd. Duemmler's Verlag, Bonn.

47. That a name is intended to convey a person's intentions can be seen in the names of popes. For when a new pope has been elected he takes a name that characterizes the direction of his ecclesiastical policies. He takes on as a symbol a name borne by an important predecessor whose policies correspond to his own inclinations. Thus he consciously and unmistakably expresses the intentions he wishes to embody in his work.

48. This sphere of life forces, which could once be reached by clairvoyant perception, has been portrayed, as already mentioned, in plant patterns in the Angiers tapestries (France, fourteenth century), interspersed with good and evil angelic beings and also a few animals. The heavenly Jerusalem also appears in this etheric sphere. Other kinds of animals are presented among the plants on the Gobelins in the Cluny Museum in Paris.

49. In 'Universitas' (H2, 1951), quoted from K.O. Schmidt, *Wir leben nicht nur einmal* (We do not live only once), Heinrich Schwab Verlag, Gelnhausen 1962, p. 62.

50. Quoted from Verbrugh (see note 32, p. 122).

51. Ibid., The out-of-the-body experience, p. 34.

52. Quoted from K.O. Schmidt (see note 49, p. 188).

53. Taken, strongly abbreviated, from Elisabeth Haich, *Einweihung* (Initiation, consecration), Drei-Eichen-Verlag, Munich, pp. 129–33.

54. In this connection we recommend the book *Geheimmnisvolles Aegypten* (Mysterious Egypt), Rascher Verlag, Stuttgart. English title: *A Search in Secret Egypt*, Rider.

55. Haich (see note 53, p. 133).
56. Taken in abbreviated form from K.O. Schmidt (see note 49, pp. 108–11).
57. From K.O. Schmidt's *Wiederverkoerperung und Karma* (Reincarnation and karma), Baum Verlag, Pfullingen 1962, p. 38.
58. From Meyer's *Encyclopaedia*, vol. 19, p. 190.
59. Kismet (Arabic) = inevitable fate, also submission to it.
60. *Die Sagen der Juden* (Jewish legends) compiled by Micha Josef Bin Gorion, Insel Verlag, Frankfurt 1962, p. 550.
61. As excavations have shown, as early as the eighth millennium BC Jericho already boasted an advanced civilization.
62. From Meyer's *Encyclopaedia* (1907), vol. 18, p. 263.
63. From G. Kolpaktchy, *Das aegyptische Totenbuch* (Egyptian Book of the Dead), translated into German with commentaries by O.W. Barth, Verlag Weilheim/Obb, 1970, pp. 115, 121, 307.
64. In fairy tales, myths and the language of the mysteries a widow is the kind of being who has lost her original spiritual principle, the masculine principle, as for instance in the well- known example of Isis losing Osiris. Where in Luke's Gospel 7:11–17 we are told of the raising of the young man of Nain and it says, in verse 12, that he was the son of a widow, this can be taken as a reference to something significant.
65. From Emil Bock, *Wiederholte Erdenleben* (Repeated earth lives), Stuttgart 1961, p. 15.
66. There is a fairy tale that tells of the animals gathering to elect their king. Although it was generally recognized that the hare was the cleverest of the animals, they nevertheless elected the bravest, and that was the lion.
67. It is also interesting to note that the writer of the Heliand (written in old Saxon in 830) expresses the idea of reincarnation in a picture (lines 3625–34): 'Jericho ... is named according to the moon ... it wanes or waxes. This is also what the human beings do here, in the Middle Realm; they depart and follow, they die old and experienced (*frode*),

become young again and return, grow to be men, until they are snatched away.

68. The hare still has in his upper jaw two large teeth for gnawing, the growth of which is constantly being replenished. These are the inner incisors, which in human beings are also pretty large. They primarily serve our speech, for when we form sounds, especially the dentals d, t, l, n, our tongue touches these. They have to do with intellectual thinking as seen from the fact that children learn to think by speaking. Also, when we think very precisely, we push the lower jaw forward, so as to put together the incisors in our upper and lower jaw. Thus we can regard the upper jaw incisors as the physionomical expression of intellectual thinking.

69. Rudolf Steiner, *Rosicrucian Wisdom*, Rudolf Steiner Press, 2000.

70. Benninghoff-Goerttler, *Lehrbuch der Anatomie des Menschen* (Textbook of human anatomy), Urban und Schwarzenberg Verlag, 1964, p. 497.

71. The word 'talent' meaning spiritual potential, very gifted, comes from the Greek word *talanton* = balance, weight, sum of money. As early as the New Testament it appears in its extended meaning of a valuable possession entrusted to someone, which then developed into having a spiritual meaning = a spiritual capacity entrusted to someone by God. Not until the twentieth century did 'talented' become the usual expression for 'gifted'.

72. Goethe, on 9 February 1788, 'Decided to be a poet not a painter' (Urachhaus Calendar 1982).

73. Carl Zackmayer wrote in his memoirs, 'as though it were a part of me' (Fischer Verlag, 1967, p. 96): 'The only healing force which can counteract this, the only support in this shifting sand is the existence of friends—the old hereditary ones who remain steadfast for decades, and also those who come suddenly, as though we had always known them, as though we had been connected with them even before birth, in an earlier life.'

74. Michaela Wolfgang Goebel, *A Guide to Child Health,* Anthroposophic Press and Floris Books.
75. Richard Nold, *Groessenzunahme, Wachstumsbeschleunigung und Zivilisation* (Increase in size, increased rate of growth and civilization), p. 28, Manz Verlag, Munich, out of print.

Hartmut Georg, 'The will to live a new life'

1. The Platonic year corresponds to the period of time it takes for the sun's position at the spring equinox to precess through all the signs of the zodiac, arriving back at the same point (25,920 years).
2. Rudolf Treichler, *Die Entwicklung der Seele im Lebenslauf* (The development of the soul in the course of life), Stuttgart 1982.
3. Rudolf Steiner, *Spiritual Guidance of the Individual and Humanity,* Rudolf Steiner Press.
4. The mucus sample taken from the secretion coming from the neck of the uterus is examined with one's actual finger and is found typically as a runny to stringy mucus in the fertile phase of ovulation, and this is backed up by the base line temperature. A graph of the temperature levels on waking can be a helpful guide to checking on the ovulation. This method requires assiduousness, experience in judging and above all going without sexual intercourse in the fertile phase. In all points there should be agreement between the partners. This method of contraception allows for constant awareness of an unborn child. It is inconvenient, and makes the greatest demands on the partners who have to make decisions constantly. But agreeing to pull together and to make sacrifices can strengthen their will.
5. Rudolf Steiner, *Spiritual Guidance of the Individual and Humanity,* Anthroposophic Press, 1992.
6. G.L. Flanagan, *Die ersten neun Monate des Lebens* (The first nine months of life), rororo no. 6605, pp. 51ff. and 63.
7. See also Werner Hassauer, *Die Geburt der Individualitaet, Menschwerdung und moderne Geburtshilfe* (The birth of the

individuality, incarnation and modern obstetrics), Stuttgart 1984.

8. Isabel Geuter Newitt, *Fuer die Eltern eines mongoliden Kindes* (For the parents of a mongoloid child), Mellinger Verlag, Stuttgart.

9. Rudolf Steiner, *Meditative Betrachtungen und Anleitungen zur Vertiefung der Heilkunst* (Meditative considerations and suggestions for deepening the art of healing), GA 316.

10. See the commendable work of Peter Petersen, *Retortenbefruchtung und Verantwortung. Anthropologische, ethische und medizinische Aspekte neuerer Fruchtbarkeitestechnologien* (Retort impregnation and responsibility. Anthropological, ethical and medical aspects of recent fertility technologies), with two further contributions by Ernst Benda and Eduard Seidler, Stuttgart 1985.

Dietrich Bauer — Postscript

1. Max Hoffmeister, *Reinkarnation, Antwort auf das Raetsel des Menschen? Eine Einfuehrung in den Gedanken der wiederholten Erdenleben* (Reincarnation, answer to the riddle of man? An introduction to the thought of repeated earth lives), Achberg 1984.
Max Hoffmeister, *Die uebersinnliche Vorbereitun der Inkarnation* (Supersensible preparations for incarnation), Basel 1979.